**Books are to be returned on or before
the last date below.**

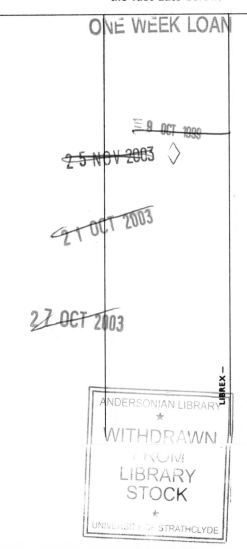

Cross-Cultural Communication

Also available from Cassell

Ken Goddard *Information Writing*
Chris Simon *Effective Communication Skills*

Cross-Cultural Communication

A Practical Guide

Gregory Barnard

CASSELL

To Sandra, Sarah and Annie,
my friends at The Cambridge Office,
and many, many others.

Cassell
Wellington House   215 Park Avenue
125 Strand   New York
London WC2R 0BB   NY 10003

© 1995 Gregory Barnard

Illustrations © Dave Haynes

British Library Cataloguing-in-Publication Data
A catalogue record for this book is available from the British Library.

ISBN 0–304–33152–X (Hardback)
     0–304–33154–6 (Paperback)

Typeset by York House Typographic Ltd, London
Printed and bound in Great Britain by Redwood Books, Trowbridge, Wiltshire

Contents

Preface

You have got half an hour to kill before catching your train or joining the throng which is heading for Gate 23 and the flight to Paris. You do not want to buy a newspaper because it will be too bulky to read comfortably on the train and, if you are flying, the chances are that you will be offered one on board. So you gravitate towards books, past the novels which you never have the time to read, and feel guilty reading even when you have the time, and you end up in front of the business books. They are very attractive these books, nicely presented and each apparently offering you the answers to many difficult questions. Maybe that one will solve your personnel problems, this one will transform you into a born leader, yet another holds the secret of sustaining a competitive edge. From a semi-consciously compiled shortlist you choose one, the one which will mean that this journey at least will not be wasted looking out of the window, or pretending to do the crossword, or reading about fish farming courtesy of the airline magazine.

Unfortunately, you have not yet grasped that, with very few exceptions, the readability of a management book is in inverse proportion to the attractiveness of the title and the famousness of the guru who wrote it. The best-selling management books require their readers to have the single-minded devotion of the marathon runner: it seems to be accepted by publishers that if you are a management guru you do not need to be able to write too; after all, your name will sell the book. Moreover, since many of the best ideas are simple ones, you have to repeat the simple ideas over and over again if you are to create a book of respectable length out of them. Then there are the diagrams – a table is worth a thousand words – and even more if you have to spend three pages explaining what the table or diagram was supposed to simplify. Add to this the fact that management theory and humour are about as inseparable as a fool and his money and you have a recipe for an unreadable masterpiece.

The belief underlying many of these books – that there is a universal solution to just about every problem that you can think of – is in itself very suspect. The greater the number of cases cited to support a theory, the more suspect the theory becomes. The life expectancy of any given management solution, in any given company, is exactly equal to the time it takes to show that it just does not work in this particular case. It is not surprising therefore that nowadays many new philosophies are condemned to failure before implementation has begun, because everybody below the CEO, or whoever the missionary is on this occasion, believes it to be the flavour of the month – to be superseded by the next one as soon as it comes out. Thus Total Quality is forgotten while Strategic Intent is on everyone's lips, which lasts until said CEO reads an article about Business Process Re-engineering, and so on.

Maybe, and it is a big maybe, if more of the books were readable, enough people within an organization would be able to read them for such books to have an effect. For, if enough people were to read the books, some of them would realize that, irrespective of the beliefs of the gurus who formulate them, these theories should not be swallowed whole. However, to be able to distil the usable from the useless or non-applicable you need to study these texts with very close attention; and how many of the management books on your shelves have you really studied rather than skimmed?

So, what have I done to guarantee the readability of the book in your hands? Let us consider first the subject matter: cross-cultural communication. I do not expect the term to set many hearts racing. However, it has one thing in its favour – relevance. Just how much relevance it has, to how many people, I hope will become clear before the end.

What is more, I am not offering a universal solution to anything. The message in this book is more along the lines of *The golden rule is that there are no golden rules*. It is my contention that all of us need to appreciate that *all* communication is, to a greater or lesser extent, cross-cultural and that it is largely because we do not recognize this fact that communication is so rarely 100% successful. I expect that the majority of those whose attention is drawn to this book will be involved in some kind of business activity with people of other nationalities. I believe that they will find some benefit in reading on; however, I would like to think that those who do not fall into this category could also gain some useful reorientation.

It was with a high degree of confidence that I asserted that the subject of cross-cultural communication was relevant to my potential readership. It is no secret that the world of business is shrinking fast and that the probability of coming into contact with a client or colleague of a different nationality is getting higher and higher in more and more sectors. In the United States of America, where nationality or citizenship is more of a religion than a question of ethnicity, the question of cultural diversity was for many years ignored, at least in terms of communication. In Britain, until recently the existence of cultural diversity would have been denied. Today, if you try to think of an area of activity which will always be carried out by local British people for local British people you will have some difficulty. Who would have

'Have you got a book on how to make foreigners less foreign?'

thought that French companies would ever control so much of Britain's water supply; or that non-British companies would hold contracts for refuse collection in British towns, or that a French company would handle the tolls on British roads and bridges.

With the globalization of more and more businesses, and the increasing relevance of cross-cultural communication, goes the increasing irrelevance of nationality. It can only be a matter of time before US and British household name corporations have executives from overseas at their helms; indeed, as I write, the 'constitution' of British Aerospace Plc is being amended to allow an American to be appointed chairman. Carnaud-Metalbox, an international company with Anglo-French roots, has a Germano-American at its head, and examples of this kind abound.

Perhaps there was once a time when universal solutions existed, when the answer could be found before the question had been asked, simply by looking in the relevant manual. Perhaps. The message of this book is that today, and tomorrow, answers can only be found after close examination of the specifics of a situation; that the answer here will almost certainly not be the answer there; that ears and eyes are better used for looking at the evidence and listening to your people, rather than reading management books and listening to gurus.

Gregory Barnard

1 The International Manager

The business which is purely national, i.e. employing people of only one nationality, buying from people of that same nationality and selling to the same, is an endangered species – and nobody is likely to try to preserve it. Within companies which have always had a degree of international exposure, managers are all the more likely to be exposed to overseas clients, colleagues or suppliers. It is not surprising therefore if the subject of the *international manager* is occupying the minds of a large number of academics, recruiters and consultants.

Does the ideal psychometric profile exist for such a manager? If it does not, how can we develop suitable managers, in terms of training and experience? For the person whose job it is to find the right manager for a key position in a large company, this speculation is of interest. However, the number of executives and positions affected by this debate is tiny in comparison with the number of managers – senior, middle and junior – who have to communicate in an international context on a daily basis, and whose success in so doing is critical to the success of their company. There seems to be far less speculation on the subject of how to pick or train these managers and directors who are not quite so visible.

Whether one is at the head of an international company or division, leading an international team, or simply participating in a team with managers of other nationalities, one's behaviour,

1

values and adherence to, or acceptance of, corporate values tacit or stated is worthy of the attention of the management development function. It is perhaps even more important that these managers should pay attention to themselves, without waiting to be told how they should be behaving, or to be developed into more effective international executives. They could be contributing not only to the smooth running of the company but of the world!

Talking to management development and training people the following four points seem to be clear:

1 Senior management accept that the concept of cross-cultural communication is one which needs to be addressed, particularly (but not only) in the context of the increasing number of cross-border mergers, joint ventures, alliances and acquisitions, but that it is not a priority for them as individuals.

2 Since senior management do not commit to developing their own cultural sensitivity, beyond attending the occasional top-level (and hence very costly) seminar on the latest theories, those immediately below them in the hierarchy do not perceive this kind of training to be a priority.

3 Without the backing of the hierarchy even the most evangelistic training managers are finding it impossible to make training happen – unless it is as a bolt-on to some existing meeting or training event, resulting in the training being reduced in value in the eyes of those participating. Whoever invented the distinction *nice to do* and *need to do* has created real problems for anyone with responsibility for the continuous development of human resources.

4 The managers who are working at the sharp end, in daily contact with overseas counterparts, are not demanding training in this very important discipline, because however great the difficulties they are

having, they reason that it is bound to be difficult when you are working with the French (the Germans, the Italians, the Taiwanese, the Japanese, etc.) and there is nothing that you can do about it. The suggestion that they are at least 50% responsible for any breakdown in communication which occurs, is likely to be met with one of a range of reactions, from disbelief to outraged disbelief.

The lack of awareness of and sensitivity to differences in culture, working practices and aspirations, has an impact on almost every aspect of business life and every normal business event: meetings, presentations, projects, sales, purchasing, managing, telephone and e-mail. From this you will gather that the managers affected are not only the jet-setting trouble-shooters. Many of those affected will never leave their offices to loiter in airport bookshops and challenge their circadian rhythms with the rigours of jet lag. Indeed, on the admittedly very dangerous assumption that travel broadens the mind, one would expect it often to be the stationary executive who is more likely to put a spanner in the communication works. This is inclined to be true not least because the stationary manager is less likely to have met his counterparts. The average manager has no automatic feeling of goodwill towards someone whom he has never met, simply on the basis that he works for the same company; and the part played by goodwill in successful communication should never be underestimated, although it very often is.

Of course there are examples of people who have established very good working relationships on the telephone or even by e-mail, but it is asking a great deal of individuals to expect them to build a rapport with someone whom they have never met. The cynic may say that meeting a counterpart does not guarantee that you will get on with him or her. This is certainly true but it is amazing how much can be achieved simply by allowing two people to meet and to share some kind of enjoyable experience, such as a well organized (i.e. orchestrated) training event. Goodwill permits the individuals concerned to overcome what had previously appeared to be insurmountable differences in character, culture or simply working practices. Distance has the effect of magnifying difference; only proximity reveals similarities and points of contact.

Meeting your opposite number also has the effect of confronting you with your inability to communicate or your weaknesses in this area, thus revealing that what you had previously thought was stubbornness or obstructiveness was simply a failure to comprehend. Like most kinds of training, success in becoming a better manager in an international context depends on the individual. The closed and narrow mind is incapable of developing itself in this way as in every other way.

In addition to the learned speculation about the ideal international manager, there is a great deal of attention being paid to the ways in which this nation differs from that, in terms of culture. How does the cultural profile of the average French manager differ from that of the average German manager and so on? This too is of little relevance to the individual, since the individual does not have to do business with the French, or the Germans, but with other individuals who are very unlikely to correspond to the theoretical average. The differences in national cultural profiles which this research appears to show is very interesting but, to my mind, quite academic. Furthermore, I am very much afraid that most of those who are drawn to read it do so for the wrong reasons; because they want to establish workable stereotypes for the people whom they are likely to meet or work with. If this research has any value for business, it is more likely to be in helping to predict difficulties which may arise during the implementation of a culture change programme, or an acquisition, or a strategic alliance. Even under these circumstances it would be far more useful, not to say indispensable, to

If you can keep your head when all about you are losing theirs –
you're an International Manager!

carry out a cultural audit of the people involved, or a sample of them, rather than to rely on the research and interpretations of someone else in another time and place. Of course it is much easier to say cultural audit than to do it. Inevitably the questions asked reflect too strongly the cultural bias of the individual/s who ask them. Very often the questions will be meaningless to the individuals of whom they are asked, and their answers will have no value.

In the chapters which follow I am to give you, the reader, a better grasp of what culture means and how differences in culture affect communication. I would like to open you up to your own culture and values and persuade you that neither is in any way absolute or universal. Lastly I would like to suggest some strategies for enhancing your ability to communicate with people of other cultures. Some of these strategies will be concrete, others will demand more of you in terms of effort, imagination and self-examination. I hope that you will be able to read this book from cover to cover and that you will feel better armed for your communicative crusades as a result. Please do not expect all the answers, because the questions have not all been asked yet and in any case there will be many which only you can answer. If, having read this book, you feel that you now know that you know nothing, I think that I will have succeeded; for I shall at least have persuaded you that, where people are concerned, a preconceived idea is an ill-conceived one.

2 Culture and Communication Defined

'If I had to begin again, I would begin with Culture' – Jean Monnet (the father of the European Community).

Imagine that you are a native of a planet where there is little or no gravity. You visit planet Earth as a tourist. You feel rather uncomfortable and you are shocked to discover that if you let go of something, it immediately falls to the ground and in many cases it breaks. This is a cause of a great deal of annoyance and embarrassment. After some time on the planet, or a few visits, you adapt your behaviour and although gravity continues to cause you inconvenience and you still appear to be rather clumsy, you fit in a little better and become less noticeable. Even if you did not expect it, gravity once noticed, is very predictable. Even if the cause remains invisible, its effect is apparent and you can very quickly relate the effect to the cause. You may not call it gravity, after all you have never heard of it; given the inconvenience which it causes you, you may think up a very uncomplimentary and a not very scientific name for it in your own language.

Many business people who travel the world as part of their job, or who spend extended periods in foreign countries, experience something similar. Many of them never get past that initial stage of shock, annoyance and embarrassment, because while they may see the effects of their clumsiness, culture – unlike gravity – is much less predictable and there is no single law of culture.

The effects too are multifarious. Perhaps nobody appreciates your prize-winning presentation, your customers do not buy your wonderful new product, in spite of your tried-and-tested sales technique. Maybe you find that the people you meet do not like you, whereas everybody warms to you at home. Your subordinates remain distant and cool towards you. People deliberately misinterpret your every message and they always turn up late to the meetings you arrange – just to insult you. Your Harvard MBA seems to count for nothing and your soundly formulated business strategies cause more amusement than even your best jokes. Your colleagues spend hours apparently enjoying meals which are clearly inedible. You just want to take the next plane home and forget all about it; and yet your company's results in the area have been really good, although WHY is a mystery to you.

On the days when you are feeling more positive you attribute your difficulties to culture and feel sure that one day soon you will wake up with the key to it in your hand.

The bad news is that there is no single key to culture. The good news is that you have most, if not all of the keys in your head.

The concept of culture

There are two key themes in this book: Culture and Communication. Both terms need to be defined before we proceed any further. One of the problems which has always dogged discussion of culture is the difficulty of arriving at a definition which encompasses all the uses of the word. In the same way that discussions about art so rarely go anywhere, because there are as many understandings of the word as there are people using it, so it is with culture. In many cases people seem to start by wanting to say something about communication between people of different nationalities and then find a definition of culture which matches or supports what they want to say.

It has become traditional in books on this subject to begin by saying what is *not* being talked about and to proceed from there. So, firstly we should make it clear that we are not talking about the kind of culture which you either have or do not have – in other words the culture of those who watch French or Italian films in the original version, who understand modern art and who sprinkle their every conversation with references as far ranging as Geoffrey Chaucer and Robert Frost, Plato and Pascal, Shakespeare and Eugene O'Neill. The kind of culture we are talking about is something far more down to earth because everybody has one.

Nor are we talking about customs, traditions or work practices, at least not to begin with, because although in many cases they result from culture, and in some cases they contribute to culture, they are external and therefore visible, at least to those who are looking. Culture is most definitely invisible. Because culture itself is invisible, but results in many visible behaviours and practices, it is quite common for us to attribute to culture all behaviours and practices which we do not understand, many of which have nothing whatever to do with it.

Take the example of the businessman who visits the French office of the multinational company for which he works. He rushes from the airport and arrives just before the scheduled beginning of his meeting, but nobody offers him a cup of coffee and no coffee is served at the meeting, at which he is the only outsider. Not knowing any better, he attributes the lack of coffee either to some unknown cultural characteristic of his hosts, or if he is feeling less than philosophical he classifies the French as rude or inhospitable. The real explanation is likely to be rather different; in France where coffee is very good and very strong, people do not drink it all day long. If they did their hearts would be palpitating and they would not sleep at night. In the UK and the US where coffee is rather different, it is practical to drink the stuff all day long and we have got into the habit of showing how hospitable we are by offering everybody a coffee as soon as they set foot on our premises.

The kind of culture which we are talking about today has been preoccupying more and more writers, thinkers and trainers since an amazing discovery was made some years ago. It was discovered that people are not all the same; different people have different values, beliefs, ambitions, etc. More or less simultaneously it was realized that some people were more different than others. Or, to put it another way, there were similarities which could exist between people; values and beliefs which could be common to a number of individuals. The name of culture was given to the sum of the values, beliefs and so on which were to be found in a particular group.

As to why we are talking about this concept of culture, it has to be recognized that, hand in hand with the realization that there are some quite fundamental differences between people and between peoples, is the acceptance of the fact that, if we are to communicate successfully, we must understand more completely the ways in which people can be different. Understanding the ways in which people can be different will lead in turn to a better appreciation of the impact on communication of these differences and, it is to be hoped, to an appreciation of how we can achieve successful communication, in spite of these differences. I have heard it said that 75 per cent of cross-border joint ventures, mergers and acquisitions which fail, do so for reasons of cultural incompatibility. An immediate benefit of better understanding of cultural issues could be a reduction in the number of failed ventures of this kind; some would not fail because they would never be attempted, being seen to be doomed from the start; others would not fail because cultural issues could be handled with greater sensitivity and a limited compatibility could be achieved.

The frustration of having a project go drastically wrong at an advanced stage for no apparent reason could become a thing of the past. The feeling that you understand what they are saying but not why they are saying it; the annoyance of seeing a presentation or training event which is enthusiastically received in the US, the UK and Holland, greeted with blank faces in France, Italy and Spain; the sheer incomprehension when you discover that the brilliant strategy which you outlined to senior regional managers is not being implemented; the bewilderment of knowing that you have achieved little or no rapport with your opposite number after months of working together closely: all of these frequently costly frustrations could be avoided or circum-vented if only you could understand where your counterparts were coming from – if you could just read their minds a little.

There have of course been many attempts to define the type of culture which we are talking about. Some of these definitions seem very attractive in that they are short and apparently con-crete; but are they accurate and are they useful?

Here are some examples of the ways in which eminent people have defined culture:

- The collective programming of the mind.

- A system of shared values and beliefs.

- The way in which a group of people solves problems.

- The way we do things around here.

The basic assumption underlying these four definitions is that culture is a group phenomenon, something which only has meaning in so far as it is shared by a group of people. This is the starting point for most of those who talk about the subject; it is also the point at which I part company from them.

I believe that culture is essentially an individual phenomenon and that if there are certain cultural similarities between people who live in close proximity to each other over a long period, then it is not entirely surprising. However, in my opinion there can be no such thing as national culture, for what can we realistically say about all, or even most, of the people of a given nationality? Who can finish the sentence: All Americans are ... or: All British people believe that. ...

The very attempt to explain culture in terms of nationalities or other groupings, or indeed the attempt to define nationalities or other groupings, comes from the overwhelming desire to stereotype, which, it seems, so many human beings feel. But perhaps it is unfair to dismiss the research of these learned and experienced people as a human response to a human need; most of the research seems to have been done by people who had a professional need to understand *groups* of people and to understand how one group of people might behave in a given set of circumstances, or how they might successfully communicate with another group. This need inevitably leads to compromise and generalization. Thinking in these terms may on occasion result in a satisfactory conclusion as far as the groups in question are concerned, but it is of little help, and frequently constitutes clear hindrance to the individual who wishes to communicate with another individual.

The truth as I see it is that there are two sides to the problem of culture. Firstly, as individuals we need to understand our own cultural identity and those of the individuals with whom we work. Secondly, as members of groups, some of us need to understand what, if any, cultural precepts are common to all, or at least most, of the individuals in our group and which cultural precepts are common to all, or at least most, of the individuals in the groups with which we have to work. I said earlier that I could not accept the concept of 'national culture'; it is, however, possible to accept that there will be a certain amount of overlap between the cultural profiles of the majority of people in a particular group, be it national or other. We have to recognize that when we speak of national culture, we can only mean a cultural profile or a list of those cultural characteristics which appear to predominate in a certain country or ethnic group.

The case for corporate culture is rather easier to make, since it is something which is either consciously or subconsciously created, and is in effect nothing but a kind of, probably temporary, cultural overlay.

Personality and individual culture

So, how can we think of culture in my terms, as an individual concept, and how does it differ from personality. Frankly I believe it to be unnecessary and undesirable to differentiate between personality and culture. When Geert Hofstede refers to the collective programming of the mind, what he is ignoring is that while there may be attempts, more or less successful, and factors, more or less influential, which move towards collective programming, the really important factor in the equation is the *mind*, and that, in every case, is individual. Therefore, anything which might be called collective programming is only likely to have a very limited significance in terms of predictable common values or behaviour at anything other than a very superficial level.

I think of culture in the following way:

Each of us is born with a glass bowl on his head, like a

goldfish bowl. When we are born the bowl is completely clear, but from then on everything we hear, see and 'learn' leaves a trace on the crystal clear surface of the bowl. The earlier we hear something and the more often we hear it, the greater the effect on our perception. Later traces, such as those left by the corporate culture mongers, will be more superficial. The result is that we can never see clearly, and we can never see as others do or indeed as another does. Even if we could find a way of taking the bowl off our heads, we could never put on someone else's bowl.

If we accept this way of thinking, we could formulate the following definition of culture:

An individual way of perceiving and responding to the world made up of values, beliefs, attitudes and preconceptions which themselves result from the effect on our individual minds of the sum total of our influences and experience.

As definitions go this one is not exactly snappy, I know, but if we return to the glass bowl analogy and think of communication as light, we can say that all communication whatever the source, will be refracted, diffused and coloured by the smeared glass bowl as it passes through. Obviously the same applies whether it is input communication or output.

You may agree with me that it would not be helpful to start discussing where culture ends and personality begins. They are very much involved with each other and since our main concern is communication and the ways in which different people perceive the world differently, it does not really matter whether we attribute these differences to culture or personality.

'What's she like? As a typist she's out of this world!'

If we are to come to terms with the fact that all people are different, we need to have ways of talking about these differences. It would not be practical, or indeed possible, to enumerate all the influences that have smeared the glass bowls of two different people. Even if it could be achieved, it would not in itself be helpful simply to list these influences, since it would reveal nothing certain about the person. For, as we have already recognized, the most important thing to consider is the interaction between the influence/experience and the individual mind. As far as predicting the behaviour in, or response to, a given situation, we need to know the result of influence/experience on the mind. It may be interesting to know why a person is how s/he is, it may make it easier to sympathize with that person, although sympathy is perhaps not the best emotion to enlist where understanding is required. While it is the domain of the sociologist and the psychologist to know *why* a person is what s/he is, for most of us it would be sufficient simply to know *what* s/he is. So we need ways of talking about culture which refer to the various constituent elements. In this way we can render differences a little more finite.

There have always been adjectives which can be used to describe individuals, or characteristics of individuals. The kinds of word we use to answer the question: What is he or she like? The areas of individuality which we focus on when answering this question will to a greater or lesser extent depend on the context in which the question is asked. If one of your colleagues asks the question about a person whom you have just interviewed for a particular job, your answer will take into account the unspoken specificity of the question, namely: How does the person score in terms of the characteristics and/or experience which you feel are required for the job. In these circumstances, your answer may include words like: practical, analytical, extrovert, discreet, honest, and so on. The problem which arises immediately is that these adjectives are much too subjective, they mean very different things to different people because, ironically, they are part of everyday language. I never thought that I would ever argue in favour of jargon, but jargon is precisely what we need if we are to discuss such intangibles meaningfully. I should explain that by 'jargon' I mean a kind of private language, in which words are chosen to convey a narrow range of meaning, in order that those who would like to discuss matters in a particular field can do so without having to rely on words which have a whole range of associations, varying from person to person, which therefore create the danger of misunderstanding.

The other potential advantage of jargon is that it may permit us to describe without judging. The jargon which we need to adopt should also be very complete, in that we need to be able to talk about all the constituents of culture, in terms of degree, tendency or presence/absence of particular constituents or dimensions. So, supposing that we wish to talk meaningfully about an individual culture, we should first establish what the prime constituents of culture are. If we think in terms of adjectives, we also need to know what their opposites are. This is not always as easy as it sounds. If, for example, we decided that honesty was one of the prime constituents of culture, we might say that the maximum score a person could have would be completely honest, or 100% honest. We also have to decide precisely what we mean by honest, and what we are saying about a person who is at the other end of the spectrum: 0% honest is not necessarily the same as 100% dishonest. If we see honesty as being a driving force, the opposite of it would be honesty not being a driving force – not *dishonesty* being a driving force.

Time for another analogy: let us abandon the glass bowls for a moment and compare an individual to a piano. The renowned American composer John Cage achieved a certain amount of notoriety with what he called the prepared piano. He would alter the sound of the piano by putting things like coins and other metal or wooden items into the piano. So, if we consider that each of us is, at birth, a perfectly tuned grand piano and that from then on everything we hear, see or experience amounts to an object being thrown into the back of the piano, the result is that the tension of the strings is affected and so is the sound of the key if an object comes to rest on it. Each key represents a dimension of culture, and the sound made when the key is played defines our position on the continuum of that dimension. Now if we compare communication with the idea of two people playing pieces of music simultaneously ... sometimes the notes will sound the same, at other times they will sound different but may complement each other. However, there will be times when the result is very dissonant indeed.

Communication

As far as definitions of communication are concerned, let us limit ourselves to saying that it is to do with *the passing of messages, the building of rapports and generally achieving as high a level as possible of mutual understanding*. One could almost include in the definition the fact that communication is never 100%. Working on communication means trying to get closer to that elusive 100%. Every constituent of culture is likely to have an impact on communication in certain circumstances; the extent to which a constituent does or does not affect communication is linked to the relative positions of the would-be communicators on the scale of this or that constituent.

What we need is a series of continua, one for each constituent of culture which we identify. The purpose of each continuum would be to permit us to position a person, and thus define them, in relation to a given cultural constituent. In this way it might be possible to say something recognizable about a person without judging them. Let us consider how this might work in relation to *time* and attitudes towards it, by looking at the case of Mr Brown:

Mr Brown is always on time, he considers that a meeting scheduled for 10.00a.m. should begin at 10.00a.m. and that any divergence from the scheduled start time is bad.

We could say that Mr Brown is very punctual. However, as a way of talking about Mr Brown's culture, the use of the word punctual is less than satisfactory for two reasons.

1 Because it suggest that his attitude to time is a positive attribute and that anyone who is different from Mr Brown in this respect is in some way worse than he is.

2 Because it is very limited in terms of what it tells us about his values

and attitudes. If, for example, Mr Brown is a station-master his punctuality can be explained as a job requirement. He may have adopted punctuality in order to meet the needs of his circumstances.

E. T. Hall addressed the issue of attitudes to time and came up with the following continuum and associated jargon:

monochronic   _____   polychronic

A brief definition, or perhaps I should say interpretation, of what is meant by these terms, which between them aim to encompass the different possible attitudes to time, is as follows:

The range of possible attitudes from *he who believes that to master one's destiny one needs to subjugate oneself to time* (monochronic) to *he who believes that to subjugate oneself to time is to lose control of one's life* (polychronic).
Immediately we need to note two riders to this definition. Firstly, the use of the word *belief* suggests a conscious decision; in fact as an element of culture, attitude to time is nearly always subconscious. Secondly, it is not uncommon for a person to have different tendencies according to the situation, e.g. a person who tends towards the monochronic at work, may have relatively polychronic tendencies at home.

Clearly Mr Brown's tendency as described above is mono-chronic. What has been achieved by coining the term monochronic is the ability to talk about a particular cultural characteristic in a way which can be understood by everyone in the same way, without passing judgement on the person who has it. The existence of a continuum from mono- to polychronic permits us to plot one element of a person's culture and then to relate it to another person's culture. For we must accept straight-away that if everyone were extremely monochronic, it would be pointless to discuss this particular aspect of a person's culture. As with all dimensions of culture, it is only of interest in that it is a way in which two people may be different, and only of interest is the extent to which two particular people are similar or different.

Attitude to time is just one of the dimensions of culture which have been identified by thinkers on this subject. We shall consider some of the other dimensions which are commonly held to exist, later in the book. What is of primary importance is the question of differences and similarities between people, which relate to one or other of the dimensions which might be called into discussion. What might be called the *Theory of Cultural Relativity* is central to any discussion of culture. With the possible exception of extreme cases, it is pointless to say of a person that they are polychronic, or highly polychronic, other than in comparison with somebody else. If we are able to create a cultural profile of an individual, its use will be to compare that individual with others, or to compare the profile with a desired profile for a given job or task, perhaps. Given a large enough database, I suppose it must be possible to give a maximum score on polychronism or monochronism; given also the ultimate in psychometric tests, it would presumably also be possible to place any individual objectively somewhere on the continuum between mono- and polychronic. Without these tools all we are likely to be able to say of a person is that they are more or less polychronic than this other person, or more or less polychronic than the norm for a particular group. That is all we can hope to do; it is also all we need to do.

Time or attitude to time, from the person who says 'No time like the present', to the person who says 'Mañana', is a dimension of culture which most people recognize once their attention has been drawn to it. How many other dimensions can be

identified which will enable us to make useful comments on an individual's culture?

One of the most important tasks which this book is setting itself is to encourage you to decide how many keys you think there are to the human piano, what they are and the extent to which they are likely to affect communication. If we can achieve this, we can then consider what an individual has to do in order to compose harmonious sonatas for two or more pianos.

Earlier I said that culture should not be confused with traditions and practices. We cannot, however, ignore behaviour in all its forms, since it is often as difficult to come to terms with and, whether or not it is a result or a cause of culture, it is likely to have an impact on the way we perceive and therefore interact with other people or peoples. In some cases traditions also serve as good examples of the fact that we do not know what we do not know. It would be impossible to guess that in some parts of the world it is considered rude to show the soles of our feet; in others one should never blow one's nose in public.

When I first visited Spain I entered a restaurant at 8.00p.m. with the intention of eating. The staff looked at me as if to say *Yes? What do you want?* I could have assumed that they had a very nonchalant approach to their profession, or that they simply did not like having to serve foreigners. After some time in the country I realized that they had simply been surprised to see me expecting to eat at that time, since most people go to restaurants at 10.00p.m. or later. Jumping to the wrong conclusion could have left me with a very negative attitude towards the Spanish. At the very least I would have assumed that it was a very unsuccessful restaurant since nobody else came in before I had finished my meal.

The main impact of collective programming seems to be that we are encouraged to jump to conclusions. I would strongly suggest that keeping an open mind means looking before you leap.

3 Other People

Although the assertion that everyone is different does not appear to be contentious, we usually behave as if we believed that everyone in a particular group was the same. Underlying the question *What are they like?* is the assumption that we know what WE are like and we want to know how THEY are different. I said earlier that there appeared to be a basic human need, or at the very least an overwhelming desire, to stereotype. Within a given nationality we call this practice 'pigeonholing'. It is when this practice is applied to a whole nationality that we more commonly call it 'stereotyping'. We all do it to a greater or lesser extent even when we recognize the absurdity of it. The need to pigeonhole or stereotype stems, I believe, from our fear of everything which we do not understand and from the fact that if we can give a name to something it becomes less threatening. If we can say that this or that person thinks or behaves in this way because s/he is French, a hippy, an accountant, mad, etc. we can then absolve ourselves of the need to consider whether they might be right, or whether their way of thinking should in some way affect us. We say to ourselves:

He behaves like that because he is French. I am not French, therefore nothing he says or does is relevant to me or can have any bearing on what I do as an American.

She does that because she is a hippy, I am not a hippy – I am a senior sales executive, therefore there is nothing that I can learn from her.

However inaccurate or imprecise our stereotypes are, they are generally based on some reality, or perception of reality. We do not have stereotypes for groups of people about whom we know nothing. Most national groups have stereotypes for other national groups which live nearby and are in some way different, and for those who perhaps live further afield and who are very different, but with whom there is some contact. Most national groups have a stereotype for another group which they have identified as being stupid. The English think the Irish are stupid and have invented many jokes based on the assumption. The very same jokes are told in France about the Belgians, in America about the Polish, in Belgium about the Dutch, in Germany about the Ostfriesians. In Northern Italy they also have the same jokes but they feature the carabinieri. All it really means is that this or that national (or ethnic, or other) group has a different way of thinking from ourselves. The characteristics which are attributed to the stereotypes generally relate to the ways in which we perceive the other group as different from us, and almost always worse than us.

The kinds of adjective which constantly recur when I ask people about their stereotypes are: stupid, mean, arrogant, disorganized and so on. It is very rare for positive qualities to be attributed to other nationalities, although it may be admitted that they have certain talents. There is a joke which begins:

Heaven is a place where –

> the police are British
> the chefs are French
> the lovers are Italian
> and everything is organized by the Germans.

That all sounds quite positive until you hear the punch line, which is:

Hell is a place where –

> the police are French
> the chefs are British
> the lovers are German
> and everything is organized by the Italians.

The fact that this joke usually gets a laugh in each of the countries cited, suggests to me that there is a grain of truth in each of the stereotypes, or at least some characteristic of each of the nationalities which each recognizes. So does this mean that these stereotypes have some use? Let's consider what they tell us in cultural terms. In order to laugh at the joke we need to believe that the Italians are passionate and disorganized, or to put it another way, erotic and erratic. Nobody really believes that all Italians are wonderful lovers, no more than they believe that no Italians have organizational ability. The grain of truth in this stereotype is that it is generally acceptable for males and females in Italy to display emotions or passion. It is not considered compulsory or even desirable for emotions to be hidden. As far as organisation is concerned we could say that in Italy order is not revered above all other things, its importance comes below that of imagination, creativity; perhaps we can also construe that there is a fundamentally optimistic view of life which tells the Italian that things will work out in the end and that bridges are better crossed when you come to them.

In opposition to the Italians are the Germans. We apparently believe that the Germans are emotionless and organized. This superficial summing up also has its merits. It is certainly true that, in professional life at least, the Germans generally consider emotions to be inappropriate, that is to say that while they would

'Ja, I know you prefer roses, Heidi, but this will last much longer.'

not deny the existence of emotions, they would prefer them to be kept out of the way. It is also unusual to find German presenters using humour to put their message across. I think we can safely make the additional generalization that order is more important to the average German than to his Italian counterpart, without suggesting that every German is a virtuoso organizer of events.

In the case of the British and the French, it has often been said that the British eat to live whereas the French live to eat. If we accept that this has some foundation in fact, we could attribute it to a process orientation among the French, as compared with a results orientation in the UK. The belief concerning the police in each country is interesting because it is very generally accepted by people of both nationalities that the British police are good and that the French police are bad. Why this should be the case is more difficult to say, but it might perhaps result from different attitudes to authority. In Britain where authority is seen as a privilege, any abuse of it is seen as a cardinal sin, in France where authority is seen as the right of the person who holds it, the way it is used is less open to question.

In summary of the above, I would say that, taken at face value, stereotypes are useless and frequently dangerous. If, however, we look beneath the surface, stereotypes can be useful indicators of some of the ways in which people can be different. Obviously I am aware that in discussing the above stereotypes I made other generalizations. In my defence I would just like to say that I do not believe that they are universally applicable, but the prevalence of certain characteristics that I perceive may help to explain why certain stereotypes persist.

As I suggested earlier, the other problem with these everyday stereotypes is that they are nearly always judgemental. They are almost always our way of saying that those people are worse than us in these respects. On the other hand, when we analyse them and start using expressions like 'attitudes to authority' and 'acceptability of emotions and their display', you will note that this quasi-scientific use of language takes away much of what was judgemental.

Now we need to work towards an enumeration of the ways in which people can be different, a list of the dimensions of culture which exist. How many keys are there to the human piano and what are their names?

E. T. Hall talked mainly about two differences, one of which was attitudes to time. The next of the greats in terms of cultural research is Geert Hofstede. Much of his work was based on four dimensions of culture, although he later added a fifth. Dr Fons Trompenaars has cited seven orientations in his more recently published work. Since Hofstede is probably the most commonly referred to authority on the subject of cross-cultural communication, let us first consider the dimensions which he puts forward as being the basis for most cultural difference. His top four are:

- Uncertainty Avoidance (high/low).

- Power Distance (high/low).

- Individual versus group orientation.

- Masculine versus feminine orientation.

In each case we are given a continuum. In the first two cases the continuum is defined, and its extremes are described simply as high and low. In the other two cases the continuum is defined by reference to its extremes.

My interpretation of the meanings of these dimensions is as follows:

- Uncertainty Avoidance (UA) refers to the degree to which one feels comfortable or uncomfortable in situations of uncertainty or instability and the way one behaves in such situations as a result of the comfort level or the way one behaves in order to avoid being in such situations.

In more simple terms, a person who is high on the UA continuum, does not feel comfortable with uncertainty and therefore generally behaves in a way which will minimize uncertainty.

A person who is low on the UA continuum feels quite at ease in situations of uncertainty and therefore does nothing to avoid it and sees no merit in any action of which the sole purpose is to render outcomes more certain.

- Power Distance (PD) is the dimension to which I referred indirectly above and concerns attitudes to authority. In a high PD corporate culture, there is a significant distance between the levels in the hierarchy. Flatter organizations are the hallmark of low PD corporate cultures.

The company in which subordinates hold their bosses in awe and where the bosses like it that way, has a high PD culture. The organization in which a team member is able to contradict the team leader in public has a low PD culture.

• Individual versus group orientation indicates the extent to which individuals feel and are encouraged to be independent or interdependent. Loyalty in the individualist culture is to number one (oneself). Loyalty in the group or collectivist culture is to a group, which will certainly be family (probably extended family) first and other groups to which one belongs after, e.g. company, team, etc. Generally speaking, poor countries reveal themselves to be more collectivist than individualist, rich countries more individualist than collectivist, although no causal connection between these facts has been established and it remains to be seen whether developing countries develop an individualist orientation along with their increasing wealth.

• Masculine versus feminine orientation relates to the importance attached to money, achievement and recognition on the masculine side, and to caring, cooperation and relationships on the feminine side.

Hofstede had access to a significant amount of data, in the form of questionnaires about values, completed by a large number of IBM employees in 50 different countries. According to Hofstede these questionnaires revealed common problems facing the employees all over the world, but solutions differed from country to country. Hofstede felt, in common with earlier researchers, that there are problems which face people all over the world and which fall into four different areas. The cultural response to these four different areas – the solutions – can be presented as four different dimensions, one for each of the areas. I do not dispute the existence of these dimensions, I am even prepared to believe that they are in some way prime dimensions. There are, however, two fundamental objections to them, as a basis for understanding culture.

1 The idea that all cultural responses to common situations can in some way be attributed to one of these dimensions, or to a combination of orientations within these dimensions, seems to me to be a massive oversimplification. Indeed, the attempt to encompass all cultural responses within these dimensions leads to a system of profiling, in terms of behaviours and beliefs, which more closely resembles a horoscope from a newspaper, than a scientific document.

This comment needs to be clarified: if you look at your country's score on a particular dimension and establish, for example, that you come from a high Power Distance culture, you then look for a profile of the kinds of behaviour and values to be expected from a person with this orientation, you will almost certainly recognize yourself. It will not be 100% you; indeed there will be some behaviours or beliefs which you do not recognize at all; but in the same way that, as a Capricorn, you will recognize yourself in a Capricorn profile if you want to, the person from a supposedly high Power Distance culture will see enough to convince them of the accuracy of the appellation if they wish to. Another relevant parallel would be the oracle at Delphi. The answers given by the oracle were always open to a wide variety of interpretations. Consequently, if you later look at the profile of the low Power Distance culture, it is just as likely that you will find behaviours and beliefs with which you can identify yourself there too.

2 The belief in national culture is not supported by the data. Although there are nationalities which score very highly on certain dimensions,

others who score very low, the vast majority of the nationalities score somewhere in between. What this tells us is not clear. What we do with the knowledge that France scores 68 on the Power Distance index, whereas Japan scores 54, is by no means obvious. Nor is the meaning of a score clear. Assuming that the scale is from 0–100 (originally it was), does a score of 68 mean that 68% of French people are high Power Distance? If so, how high? Does it mean that most French people are relatively high Power Distance? If so, what is meant by most French people? What, in fact is meant by relatively high?

In discussions with Human Resources managers and Training Managers and others who had an interest in being able to predict cultural behaviours, those who had studied the subject very frequently said: 'Yes, I have read Hofstede, I'm familiar with the model, but what do you do with it?' I believe that, at least in part, this frustration resulted from the fact that these indices tell us nothing concrete about a group of individuals, let alone one individual.

Nonetheless, there is a great deal which is of value in the work of Hofstede, and few people who have looked into the matter would deny that there is a clear tendency towards the high Power Distance within French companies, as compared with British or American ones. Unfortunately, human nature is such that even when we use such neutral terms as Power Distance we manage to be judgemental. The British manager speaking of the French is quite capable of criticizing them for being so high Power Distance. However neutral a description appears to be, when it is describing the way in which a person or a people is different from oneself or one's own, it very rapidly becomes a way of criticizing.

The fact that these dimensions are used to describe differences between nationalities means that they are stereotypes; the attempt to make them useful by being unemotive and non-judgemental fails; the fact that they only have limited accuracy means that they fail on that count too. their value lies in the fact that they are not superficial in the way that everyday stereotypes are. They are genuinely analytical and move us along the road towards knowledge of how people can be different. Furthermore, although the accuracy is limited, if we have to talk about orientations within a particular national group, Hofstede's work offers us a much safer way of doing it and provides us with some useful information on which to base predictions about likely behaviours, responses and so on.

My opinion that his work does not support a belief in the concept of national culture means that the principal value of his work for my purposes is his identification of four dimensions of culture. To go forward from this point we need to consider the other dimensions of culture which have been identified.

Other dimensions of culture

Dr Fons Trompenaars, in his book *Riding The Waves of Culture*, speaks of seven different orientations. One of the seven is presented as being the opposition of Universalism and Particularism. For Dr Trompenaars the difference between the two is as follows:

The Universalist believes that there are absolute rules which always apply irrespective of circumstances and situations.

The Particularist believes that more important than absolutes are the obligations of relationships and unique circumstances.

Dr Trompenaars' definition of the particularist orientation is in fact rather narrow. He seems to say that the unique circumstances which form the basis for decisions in a particularist culture are always connected with friendships or relationships. I contend that the belief that your relationship with a person will always dictate how you behave is a kind of Universalism. In other words you believe in the absolute importance of relationships. To my mind, the particularist – whose existence I readily admit – is the person for whom there are *no* absolutes, decisions being based on the interplay between circumstances, relationships and a host of other variables.

Dr Trompenaars quotes a series of exercises which he uses to establish the orientation of a person on this front, or to illustrate the existence of the two extremes. One of the exercises puts the participants in the following situation:

You are in a car driven by a close friend. S/he is driving at 50 mph in an area where the speed limit is 30 mph. The car hits a pedestrian. Your friend's lawyer tells you that if you will testify that your friend was driving at 30 mph, s/he will avoid a prison sentence. There are no other witnesses or evidence.

Questions: Would you lie to save your friend? Yes or No.

Does your friend have any right to expect you to protect him/her?

For Dr Trompenaars, the person who says 'No', is showing a Universalist orientation, because they are obeying what they see to be an absolute rule: You must not lie. Whereas the person who says 'Yes', is displaying a Particularist orientation, since their belief in the importance of friendship overrules all else.

I run a similar exercise, with one major difference. I allow for a third answer: *It depends*. The person who answers *'It depends'*, does so because they need more information on which to base their decision. Because they do not believe in absolute rules, neither *You must never lie*, nor *You must always help your friends*: they need more information. The information which they need may not always be the same; the way they respond to the information which they receive may differ. They resemble each other only in so far as they dismiss the automatic response which is possible for the Universalist.

To summarize, both the answer 'Yes' and the answer 'No', indicate a Universalist orientation according to my interpretation. Only the person who says '*It depends*' is revealing a particularist tendency.

In other similar exercises Dr Trompenaars shows that, in any case, the orientation which one apparently displays does depend on the unique set of circumstances. Those who displayed a particularist tendency in the exercise above, may display universalist tendencies in other circumstances. In another exercise the participant is told to imagine that s/he is a restaurant critic who has just visited a new restaurant into which a close friend has sunk all of her capital. The restaurant is very poor in the estimation of the critic and s/he is asked if they would go easy on the friend in their article. This situation drew very different responses, notably from the French participants, who clearly felt that any rule which might relate to friendship was overruled when it came to serious matters like food (or perhaps professional integrity).

It seems to me that we are taught several things by these further exercises:

• The importance of the interplay between the different dimensions of culture cannot be overestimated.

• If we cannot be confident of extrapolating the behaviour of an individual from his/her apparent orientation, how can we hope to predict the responses of a nationality with any accuracy?

• Most people's orientations (*vis-à-vis* all cultural dimensions) are likely to be closely linked to the circumstances in which they find themselves.

'So that's boiled beef with a julienne of spring vegetables on a coulis of sun-dried tomatoes with basil, followed by steamed pudding complemented by a vanilla-scented crème anglaise.'

This last point means that any attempt to pigeonhole peoples or individuals is likely to be frustrated and should therefore be avoided. Whichever definition of culture we take, it is clearly a dynamic thing, something which can be changed and is likely to develop. However constant we may feel our own culture to be, or want another's culture to be, we have to face the fact that every new situation not only is perceived in accordance with one's cultural perspective but also contributes to that cultural perspective. We have to get away from the idea that people and peoples are constant. After all, if we really believed in it what would be the sense in trying to instigate any of the cultural change programmes which are so popular in so many companies nowadays?

Individual stereotypes are not only dangerous in that people change over time, but also in view of the fact that a person's orientation in relation to the various cultural dimensions may vary with different sets of circumstances, e.g. at home/at work. We cannot assume that a person who reveals a tendency towards high Power Distance when responding to one set of questions, will constantly reveal the same tendency when the questions, or the parameters are changed.

4 How People Differ

So having agreed that *everyone is different*, we can perhaps begin to understand these differences if we start close to home and consider the differences which exist between people of the same nationality, and even of very similar backgrounds and education in the broadest sense.

The phrase: 'My wife does not understand me' will be familiar to most people reading this book; if we ignore the reasons for which it is most often said, i.e. as a pretext for transgressing one's marital vows, and consider what it really means, it may be revealing.

Let us begin by dismissing the proposition that the person speaking is an English-speaking non-linguist whose wife does not speak English. We shall assume that the speaker and his wife are both of the same nationality and mother tongue. What does the husband mean when he says: 'My wife does not understand me?' In many cases he will mean that he and his wife do not share the same beliefs, values, ambitions. Perhaps he is a simple man with simple objectives, while his wife is very ambitious. Maybe he is a dynamic and ruthless achiever and his wife has strong religious principles. Major sources of irritation are often very minor events which highlight more significant differences. Divorces have resulted from the fact that one partner is never punctual, one partner squeezes the tube of toothpaste in the middle, one partner drinks milk out of the bottle or dunks his

' . . . and when you say that price is not important Madam, does that mean . . .?'

toast in his tea. At another time it may be worth considering what cultural characteristics result in one person squeezing the tooth-paste tube in the middle and another finding this behaviour intolerable in the long term.

Of course what one person is or isn't, does or doesn't, is not in itself as important as how what they are or what they do differs from the people with whom they have to regularly interact or communicate. You are only called unpunctual by someone who is more punctual than you, and for whom punctuality is import-ant. What is considered informal at the gentlemen's club may be considered overdressed at a barbecue.

The man who says: 'My wife doesn't understand me', is probably saying that due to a fundamental difference in values, beliefs and so on, communication between the two of them is significantly less than 100%. The words he uses to express this are in fact quite accurate, because language is nothing unless the words have values attached to them; when two words or more are used together, a difference in the values attached to them by the two people communicating becomes more significant.

Almost any two people could agree a definition of words like important, cheap, education, and clothes. However, as soon as these words are paired difficulties may arise. Two people can agree that education is important without thinking the same thing, even if they have previously agreed definitions of *education* and *important*. If two people are discussing clothes and one of them says to the other that a particular jacket is cheap, even if they have previously agreed a definition of cheap, they may not agree on the cheapness of the jacket. Nor is it only money that can cause disagreement. In fact we are discussing cases which should be relatively safe, in that in these cases the people concerned have agreed on definitions of the words they are using. In real life we find that most people do not share or agree 100% on the definitions of the words which they use to communicate. When one person says to another: ' . . . and make sure it's done properly', he or she does not normally enter into a discussion on the precise meaning of 'make sure' or of 'properly'.

Listen in to this conversation between a husband and wife:

Wife: 'We've got to go to Sainsbury's this morning.'

Husband: 'Why?'

Wife: 'Why do you think?'

This brief conversation, ending in a rather impatient, perhaps irritable remark, demonstrates the inefficiency of language when it is left to its own devices. The question 'Why?' which is central to it, could mean several different things. The wife assumes that it is asking a question which does not need to be asked, i.e. 'Why do we have to go to the supermarket?' Answer: 'To buy food'.

In fact it could be asking any of the following questions:

Why we?

Why Sainsbury's?

Why this morning?

Why have to?

The husband asking the question is annoyed by the response, because it assumes that he is asking a needless question. His wife should know that he is not in the habit of asking such ill-considered questions and should therefore have asked herself which of the other possible questions was intended.

It is not surprising that people often conclude that they are not speaking the same language. For here we have an example of two people who have a great deal in common, including language, and yet who are finding it difficult to get to the end of a very simple exchange without misunderstanding occurring. Furthermore it is very difficult to apportion blame. The wife has perhaps a tendency to assume that her husband always knows what is meant – even when it is not said – but is often deliberately obstructive. The wife could have been more explicit, although she thought the statement was simple and clear enough. The husband too could have been more explicit:

Why is it necessary for both of us to go?

Why do we have to go to Sainsbury's as opposed to the shop down the road?

Wouldn't it be possible to go this afternoon or tomorrow?

Why is it necessary; surely we have what we need already?

The failure to communicate described above does not even have a genuine cultural basis to it. As soon as we bring culture in, the danger of communication breakdown, already significant, is greatly increased.

So what does culture mean when we are comparing two or more people of the same nationality? What are its constituents and how is it likely to impact on communication? We do not need a new definition of culture to talk about it in intra-national terms; it is still the sum of values, beliefs, etc. Hofstede tells us that, according to development psychologists, by the age of ten a child is in possession of most of his/her basic values. Consequently we can look to the parents and the environment in which the child spent his/her first ten years, to identify the source if not the nature of their values. Family, religion, education, socialization are all factors which will contribute to the cultural definition of the ten-year-old, and of the adult. An unknown Jesuit is once though to have said: 'Give me a child at the age of seven and he is mine for ever'. If we are to believe both Hofstede and the Jesuit, the vast majority of the development of a child's cultural make-up/values system, happens between the ages of seven and ten. However, even if we could imagine the existence of two children with identical experience at this age, we could not assume that they would even be similar in adulthood; values and beliefs form a kind of conscience – and just as two tax inspectors may come up with different tax computations for a given individual, by applying two different sets of criteria (both of which are valid and known to each of them) one's culture in later life will largely depend on how and when one applies the values and beliefs which one has adopted (or is it the values and beliefs which adopt us?).

Early influences

Although knowing what the influences on an individual have been will not enable us to create a cultural profile of him/her, the knowledge may nonetheless be enlightening in that it may reveal the depth or irreversibility of cultural characteristics which have been identified by observation. If, for example, we have discovered that an individual is anti-alcohol, finding out that his natural father was an alcoholic, his much respected step-father was a member of the Plymouth Brethren, that he works as a lay-preacher in the Mormon Church and has been employed for many years in a large American multinational which bans all alcohol from company premises, we can be fairly sure that his attitude is not going to be changed by you saying: 'Go on, just have one, it'll put hairs on your chest!'

The principal influences in early life are likely to be family based. The number of children in the family, the culture of the parents, attitudes to education, wealth or otherwise, the geographical location of the family home – which country, inner city or provincial, etc. – all of these factors may be decisive one way or the other. We are never likely to know what the parents told him or her never to do, or what always to do, but these pieces of advice do tend to linger. If your mother regularly said to you that her father always said to her: 'Never trust a man who wears suede shoes' – even if you dismissed the advice as ridiculous years ago, you probably still notice if one of the candidates for the job as your assistant is wearing suede shoes; and if you are looking for a way of differentiating ...

As I said, knowing about a person's background does not tell you anything certain about the person. The daughter of devout Catholics may grow up to be a devout Catholic, or a moderate Catholic, or an atheist, or a Muslim convert. I would suggest that it is unlikely that she will become a Protestant or adopt the Jewish faith, but you never know. The only child of wealthy parents may grow up despising money or worshipping it, respecting it, or squandering it, even being indifferent to it.

Wealth and religion are powerful but unpredictable influences. In the West, religion has gradually become rather a peripheral matter for most people. The term 'devout' is in the process of being replaced by the pejorative 'fundamentalist'. What this means is that it is becoming less and less acceptable to allow any other God than Mammon into everyday life. When I was at school, a private Roman Catholic boarding school, I remember being very impressed by the words of a song by the band Jethro Tull. The song, entitled *My God*, contained the words 'He's not the kind you have to wind up on Sundays'. Today, if you wind your God up more than once a year you invite suspicion. We were not always thus, which is worth remembering next time you encounter Islam.

Education, private or state, and the amount of support given and value attached to it by parents, and of course one's level of success, will contribute significantly to one's culture and world view in later life. In the case of higher education the subjects studied have a major part to play. The study of a science is likely to have a radically different effect from the study of an Arts subject. Study at Ivy League colleges in the United States, Oxford and Cambridge in the UK and their equivalents world-wide, leaves its mark in more ways than one.

After formal education is 'complete' we may encounter strong influences from the sector or profession which we enter. Although it will often be the case, we cannot assume that it is a person's culture which has dictated their choice of sector or profession. Just as often culture will simply have made us discount the possibility of embarking on certain careers. There must, however, be examples of born accountants who are working in advertising, and born industrialists who are working as doctors, and so on. The interplay of cultural characteristics which are well established, with sectoral influences which appear to clash, may produce results which are even less predictable than the average.

How then can we illustrate culture clash within a given nationality, within a given home? The four principal dimensions used by Hofstede are associated primarily with workplace values and beliefs. He does, however, provide indications of how different tendencies may manifest themselves within the home. A parent who scores high in terms of Power Distance is likely to expect unquestioning obedience from his/her children. The children may turn into adults who have the same expectations; then again they might react against this attitude and be determined to treat their children as equals from an early age. Whichever case we take they will probably be married before they discover the tendency of their husband/wife. In cases where the parents have opposing tendencies there is a great deal of potential for conflict, particularly where one parent is encouraging the children to question everything which they do not understand, including instructions and rules. We can probably assume also that the high Power Distance father feels that he is head of the family and can expect a similar level of compliance from his wife. The high Power Distance wife may be inclined to accord such obeisance to her husband whether he expects it or not. I have recently heard that in a large banking organization in the UK, in which there are very few women managers in senior positions – in spite of the fact that women represent a good percentage of managers at lower levels – when asked why they did not apply for more senior positions, many women responded that it would not be right for them to occupy a more senior or better paid position than their husbands. It would be interesting to know how the husbands would react if they discovered that their wives felt this way, and how many of them would actually approve or even assume it to be the case.

Different attitudes to time are often the cause of marital conflict too. They also provide us with a good example of how people can apparently know each other without understanding.

'No, I won't be long.'

Thus while the war-torn veteran of many international meetings may be able to predict with a high degree of certainty how long negotiations will last, or at what point they will break down, he or she may be at a loss to explain these vicissitudes to the new assistant other than by saying: 'That's the French for you,' or perhaps 'It's down to the Mexican culture'.

When Mr Jones goes out on Saturday morning to buy a new screwdriver from the hardware store in the nearby town, Mrs Jones knows that he will not be back for hours. However, she does not know why he will be gone so long, or what is going through his head as the 45 minute task moves into its third hour; consequently she is unable to predict the occasion when he will come back in only 45 minutes. The more important consequence is that she continues to hope that he will be back soon and she continues to be angry when he is not. Of course, one cannot say why Mr Jones takes so long; it could be for any number of reasons, as many reasons as there are Mr Jones's. Perhaps he feels a slave to time all week and therefore relishes the opportunity to exercise power over a small portion of it. He may feel that time spent in contemplation without domestic distractions is well spent. He may use the time congregating with other errant husbands over a beer. Searching for inspiration for a gift for his wife's birthday – only three months away – could also explain it. What prevents every Mrs Jones from understanding every Mr Jones is the fact that he is doing something which she never does. She could never justify to herself spending an extended period of time with no visible result and therefore cannot understand that someone else might have no difficulty with such justification.

Team management

Management today very often involves participating in cross-functional teams long before you get to the ultimate cross-functional team which is the board of directors. To say that a team of this sort contains people with different cultural make-ups may seem like a truism. Inevitably when you represent a particular function you bring with you the concerns and priorities, values and beliefs of that function. Yet this fact is too often ignored as people tell themselves that they all share the priority of making money and being successful and any difference in culture resulting from a distinct functional background is only an overlay on the mind of a responsible, intelligent and competent individual. This oversimplification can prove disastrous. After all, it is not generally a coincidence if you have arrived at a position of authority within a given function. If you have responsibility, it is probably because you are good at your job, if you are good at your job, it is probably because you have been doing it for some time; if you have been doing it for some time, it is probably because it suits you; if it suits you, it is probably because your own cultural make-up represents a good match with the values and beliefs which support the priorities of that function. A given cultural profile which has been reinforced by years of working within a given function will often result in an individual who is blind to the logic of others.

Consider the following situation:

Directors from company X are meeting to discuss a proposal for investment in state-of-the-art technology which will enable them to produce a brand new product range at very competitive prices. The product range is quite revolutionary but market research strongly suggests that it will be a winner. Attending the meeting are the Managing Director, the Financial Director, the Production Director and the Marketing Director. As a marketing-led company, in which marketing costs represent 40% of all costs, on the retirement of the Managing Director it has always been the Marketing Director who steps into his shoes.

Chairing the meeting the MD asks the Production Director Doug Smith to begin:

Smith: (a highly qualified engineer who nonetheless feels that he is not taken seriously by the others because of his relatively unglamorous job and who resents the fact that he always seems to be the last in line when money is to be invested):

To be honest, David, I'm amazed that we are even talking about this new line. If there is any money available it is because of profits on existing lines and those profits come about because I am constantly being told to drive down production costs. I have to contend with mounting maintenance costs on

*out-of-date machinery and live in constant fear that a major
breakdown will throw our scheduling into chaos. I think we
should be updating our technology for existing lines which are
tried and tested and profitable, rather than spending a fortune
on the whims of the whiz kids.*

Next to speak is the Marketing Director, James Digby.

Digby: (a recent MBA has convinced him that he is the only one
with the ability to see the big picture; however he is a marketing
man through and through having joined X after five years in the
marketing department of a major consumer goods multinational; he knows that the MD is likely to retire within two years
and is concerned that he may be considered too young to take his
place):

*I appreciate your concern about existing machinery and lines,
Doug, but aren't you missing the point? Standing still means
going backwards. We have to grow to survive in the world
today; furthermore we are discussing money which has been
earmarked for development not consolidation. This proposal
represents an opportunity to corner a new market, but one
which we understand and thereby to make up for the relative
lack of success that we've had in new markets in recent years.
In any case, if our predictions are even half right we'll have
more than enough money to buy you your new toys within two
years.*

After Digby, the MD calls upon John Cashmore, the Financial
Director.

Cashmore: (as the longest-standing director in the company,
having taken up the post three years before the current MD
became the marketing director, Cashmore's opinion is always
appreciated, although the others also realize that he tends to be

rather cautious and to behave as if the money were his own; he is at least five years away from retirement):

As you know, it is some time since we have been in a position to consider an investment of this size, largely because of our costly attempts to enter markets which were outside our experience. If we are able to consider it today it is mainly a result of sound financial controls and the restraint of Doug and others. With interest rates so low there is not much point in hanging onto cash, but that does not mean that we should go on an ill-considered spending spree. I am not yet sure why James is so convinced that we are on to a winner with this one, particularly in view of the fact that he was just as enthusiastic about our last little venture. I would need more evidence of the size of this new market as well as of our ability to exploit it, before I could endorse this proposal.

At this early stage in the discussions there are no surprises. Each of the directors is speaking from his own point of view, putting forward his concerns based on the priorities of his function. It is not necessarily easy to arrive at a decision but we have no reason to suppose that the proposal, which will require the cooperation of all departments, will be deadlocked. However, if we create cultural profiles for each of the directors we will have a clearer idea of any trouble which may lie ahead.

Cultural profiles

Doug Smith thinks of the production team as a family. From his assistant down to the factory cleaners they are his children and he is very protective of them. He respects their input and praises and criticizes easily. He does not expect his decisions to be questioned by them and even if a decision is imposed on him by the board he carries it through as if it were his own. At first he was not comfortable speaking his mind to the MD, but he is encouraged to do so and tends to be rather blunt when expressing himself. He is a practical man and does not see the need for diplomacy. He is a strong believer in planning and hates surprises, but will support innovation if he believes that his team will benefit by it. He understands that profit is very important but for him it is not everything. He distrusts individualists and anybody who does not know how to listen. He prefers to concentrate on one task at a time, always arrives on time for meetings and is likely to leave before the end if the meeting drags on. He takes criticism of his own work philosophically but does not like criticism of members of his team.

James Digby considers himself to be a creative, modern manager. He reads management books and is likely to swallow new theories whole, without properly digesting them. Production for him is a necessary evil and he is glad that the factory is several miles away. Business means taking risks and he loves to do so. He is less inclined to take risks where his career is concerned. He has a more flexible attitude to time and often arrives late for meetings, and takes calls during meetings. He does not mind being kept waiting as he always has work with him. He loves juggling several projects at the same time. He encourages participation in decision-making by his team, but will often overrule them. At meetings he tends to speak for longer than anybody else. He believes in doing extensive market research but trusts his instincts above anything else. He would like to be more diplomatic but gets frustrated if things are not going his way. He does not like criticism of his work because he does not separate himself from his work. He is more interested in turnover and market share than in profit.

John Cashmore has no faith in instincts or intuition. If it cannot be counted it does not exist. He has a great deal of faith in ratios and can always come up with apparently irrefutable evidence against projects with which he does not agree. He has more self-confidence than any of the other directors and privately thinks of them as his children. With very few exceptions he thinks of the members of his own team as sophisticated though not 100% reliable calculators. He usually says what he thinks in a diplomatic way and ignores or does not notice implications made indirectly by other speakers. He never takes sides and does not need allies. He always arrives at 8.00a.m. precisely and always leaves at 6.20p.m. He is almost never late for meetings and stays until the end, but he does not appear to notice if others arrive late.

Although the above profiles may seem rather caricatural, they do represent recognizable people with recognizable differences. Furthermore, I do not think that any reader would conclude that these directors were of a particular nationality. With the exception of their names, nothing about the directors described above would suggest that they were probably of this nationality, or probably not of that. We can quite readily assume that they are all of the same nationality and that there is no way of knowing which. Most of the differences stated or implied correspond to the dimensions discussed earlier and defined by Hofstede. We do not know *why* they are how they are, although we might suspect that their function has had an influence; nor does it really matter why. It is only important to know how they are and how they differ – and to understand something about the nature of these differences.

Irrespective of how accurate such profiles might be, it is clear that they are not complete; obviously much more could be said about these individuals, much could be added which would contribute to an understanding of how well or badly they are likely to communicate. If we try to develop a profile of a given nationality using the research of Hofstede, we might well end up with something similar to one of the above profiles. As profiles of individuals, though incomplete they may be considered useful. To impose such a profile on a whole nation or on all the managers of a given country is patently absurd. None of the academic treatises – be they socio, semio, psycho or anthropo – offers a logical approach to communication, in that each of them suggests ways in which you can decide how to communicate with a person whom you have never met.

However it is only when we begin to understand how people might be different, what fundamental beliefs they might hold which are radically different to our own, that we can begin to devise ways of communicating with them more successfully. Bearing in mind that there are an infinite number of individuals with whom we might have to communicate at some stage, of the same nationality or another, it seems clear that it would be easier to begin with the other side of the equation. Who or what am I? What are my fundamental beliefs?

If the first value of the academic books on culture is that they give us an idea of how people might be different from us, their second value is that, by setting out some of the dimensions of culture, they enable us to start thinking about culture as it might be applied to ourselves, to focus on our own individual culture. Just as it is extremely difficult to answer the question: 'What do you want for Christmas?' unless some of the options are laid out, in the same way, trying to establish a profile for ourselves without some benchmark is a most difficult task. It must be more logical, though, first to create a profile of the one person whom we can study or analyse at our leisure, namely the person known modestly in certain cultures as *number one*: oneself. It would be highly dangerous to assume that we know ourselves, in cultural terms at least. We may think we know how we would react in certain sets of circumstances; we may even be right. It is unusual to know why we would react in a given way. In my experience there are a great many people who believe themselves to be easy-going, who are anything but. These people could continue thinking that they are easy-going until they meet somebody who fervently believes the opposite of what they fervently believe themselves. Indeed, the more fervently we believe something, the more difficult it is to imagine that someone else may believe the opposite.

Creating a profile for oneself demands a kind of out-of-culture jump. It has to be done in a very dispassionate way by listing as many dimensions of culture as we recognize – we do not need the permission of the experts to establish new categories, or dimensions; as I have suggested above, I do not believe that we should restrict ourselves to Hall's two dimensions, Hofstede's four (or five), or Trompenaars' seven orientations – each dimension should have two extremes and one should ask oneself how completely one agrees or disagrees with the values or attitudes or beliefs which embody or express these dimensions. It may well be that in many cases we will find ourselves more or less agreeing with a given value statement. In order to verify how we really are, we need to check ourselves against the opposite value. If we can honestly say that the opposite extreme is not shocking to us, then we are probably in a relatively safe middle ground. There are doubtless many different ways of establishing one's cultural profile but it is likely to be made up of every value, belief, source of motivation, etc. which might affect decisions made at work, positions adopted *vis-à-vis* others, or approaches to communication. We may wish to group them in terms of depth of feeling, perceived source, or the extent to which they define us as people. We should not, I suggest, discount any purely on the basis that it may stem from the same root as another. The important thing is to be able to imagine what the opposite of each element is/would be.

As suggested earlier in the book, relativity is the only important concept. We can only consider ourselves to be different in relation to a given, other individual. This process of identifying what we believe, perhaps why we believe it, and accepting that this belief is not universally accepted as true or right, can be quite a painful one. However, apart from the fact that it is quite obviously the best way to start understanding culture and what motivates people, if you cannot analyse yourself – with the headstart provided by having access to your own head and knowledge of your own experience – you cannot be too optimistic about your chances of analysing other people when you meet them and start working with them. When you come to consider why your counterpart behaves the way s/he does and how best to communicate with him/her, there will be a whole history of which you will be unaware and which you may never even touch the surface of. You may think that one individual's experience in a developed country is not going to differ radically from the experience of another individual in any other developed country; but you would be wrong. You simply do not know what you do not know, nor can you, in most cases, guess at it. You may for example never discover that your Japanese counterpart underwent a month's training when he entered his company, during which he was required to learn a whole manual of DOs and DON'Ts relating to how to behave in the company. It does not happen in every Japanese company, I only know for certain of one; but who would have guessed it? The list of differences in terms of experiences, beliefs and values which may exist is a very long one and most of the differences just cannot be guessed at.

Even with the help of the eminent researchers into culture, you may find it difficult to establish how many keys there are to the human piano of which you are an example. It may help to consider the emotions which you most commonly or most strongly experience. What makes you angry, sad, happy, relaxed, ashamed, proud, uneasy, embarrassed, frustrated, content, grateful, bitter, excited or bored? What motivates or demotivates you? What is important to you and what is of no importance? What do you fervently believe and what do you just as fervently refute? To complement the cultural factors which you establish in this way, you may find it useful to ask the same questions of someone who is near to you, your partner or a colleague – in any case someone whose testimony you can verify from your personal experience of them. If you do not discover anything about yourself which surprises you, it probably means that you are not digging deep enough, looking far enough and you may need to enlist the help of someone who knows you well.

In discussion with friends and fellow culture vultures Nigel Ewington and David Trickey of The Cambridge Office, a training organization based in Cambridge (UK), we arrived at a figure of 18 cultural precepts which we felt did not overlap each other too much and which we had identified, in some extreme form, either in ourselves or in other people. They are all factors which are likely to affect the way in which we communicate, what we choose to communicate and the extent to which we are likely to succeed in communicating – depending of course on the cultural profile of our interlocutor. Nor did we feel that we had exhausted all the possibilities. Some of them, admittedly, are based on what others call dimensions or orientations, but they also included:

Being v Doing, i.e. the extent to which we do, or don't identify ourselves with what we do. Do we consider a criticism of our work to be a criticism of ourselves – or not?

Efficiency v Effectiveness, i.e. do we focus on processes, or only on results. Might we be inclined to say the end justifies the means, or it is better to travel hopefully than to arrive?

Pessimist v Optimist, i.e. do we concern ourselves more with weaknesses and threats than with strengths and opportunities or vice versa?

Each of these precepts, as we have chosen to call them, constitutes a framework for conflict or tension when you consider how difficult it would be for two people at opposite ends of any of these continua to work together, irrespective of their nationalities. If you add to the equation different mother tongues, different learned working practices and any other differences which may occur as a result of being of different nationalities, what seemed to be difficult may appear to be impossible.

Having completed this exercise in self-analysis, your next step is to consider why you are who you now know you are. If you neglect this part of the process or satisfy yourself that you are not the product of your experience and influences, you may be tempted to believe quite simply that you are right and that everyone else is, in a variety of ways, wrong. Resist this temptation and it may, in some cases, be possible to identify factors or influences from your past to which responsibility can be attributed; conversely it may be that your profile seems to have come about in some random haphazard way. In either case you must accept that things could easily have been different and that there is therefore nothing sacred, absolute or universal about your perception of the world and its ways.

5 How People Can Be the Same

Before moving on to suggest ways in which you can boost your chances of winning the battle to communicate, I feel I need to address the question of similarities between people of a given nationality. We have acknowledged that there is likely to be a grain of truth in stereotypes; we know that in some countries certain forms of behaviour are acceptable, even desirable, but which are considered unacceptable in other countries.

There are dozens of books, many of them written in the past five years, which attempt to create a science of culture; by positing the existence of a limited number of cultural character-istics and then attributing different scores to different countries based on answers given to questionnaires, nearly all of them compiled by people who come from similar (by their own defini-tion) cultures. Earlier in the book I suggested that this trend stemmed from a universal human need for stereotypes, although if I were so inclined, I could attribute this desire to universalist tendencies on the part of this new breed of culturologists. Following on naturally from the new discovered discipline of What is a Frenchman? What is a German? What is an American? is the even newer study of What made the Frenchman what he is? What made the German what he is? and so on. In this area of study the game consists of explaining why a given nationality has the cultural profile which you have previously decided that it has.

'The British are all the same

'Explanation' is perhaps not the most accurate word I could use here, since it generally appears to be sufficient to show that what you say is true today, was also true yesterday and even two, three or even four hundred years ago. 'Show' is perhaps not the most accurate word since it generally appears to be sufficient to find a quotation from somebody who wrote many years ago and who says something which mirrors what you believe to be true today. One can then apparently say not only that a certain medieval philosopher's words show that a particular nationality has always had certain tendencies, but also that they have these tendencies because of a certain medieval philosopher.

However, even if we accept that there is good evidence that a way of thinking which existed hundreds of years ago is prevalent today, what do we say about the French people – for example – who do not think this way? If 62 per cent of French managers think a certain way, that may contrast starkly with only 40% of Americans, but it still means that 38% of French managers think differently. If your research has explained why the French are 62% *this*, it most certainly does not explain why 38% of them are *that*.

All that the culturologists can hope to demonstrate with their historical analyses, is that most people behave a certain way because most people have always behaved in this certain way. This is quite easy to believe since any value or belief which is held, and held to be important, by even a small number of influential people, is likely to have an impact, over a period of time, on the state education system and therefore to be self-perpetuating.

There is, I believe, a range of chicken-and-egg type questions which can be asked.

For example:
Is this or that prevalent belief or behaviour a result of the education system, or does the education system reflect the prevalence of the belief or behaviour?

Perhaps even more important is the question:

Are things usually done in this way because of a prevalent cultural characteristic, or is there a prevalent cultural characteristic which results from the fact that this approach is generally adopted.

Of course we cannot ignore the possibility that we are making a mistake in trying to establish a connection between the behaviours in a given country and the cultures of individuals in that country. Given that things have to be done in one way or another, and given that the way adopted is likely to be the way that things have been done before, it is presumably possible that, in any given place, things are done like this because they are done like this.

Many of the questionnaires which have been used to establish cultural profiles ask questions the answers to which reveal more about how things are done than how an individual might have chosen to do things had there been no precedent. However accepting of change an individual may be, s/he is always likely to favour a response which reflects his or her *status quo*. In other words, the fact that a particular approach to management has always been the norm in a particular country, company or division, does not allow one to assume that this approach reflects the underlying cultural make-up of all or even most of the individuals in that unit. Nor does it allow us to assume that an attempt to introduce a different approach is doomed to failure. We must, on the other hand, be aware that any attempt to change what has always been the *modus operandi* in a given unit, is likely to encounter some resistance. We cannot assume, in any circumstances, that the fact that the CEO and his favourite management guru believe a particular way of working to be desirable will be enough to make everyone willingly change the habits of a lifetime.

If we relate this to a specific set of circumstances it may be easier to draw a conclusion. If we are to believe Hofstede, the French have a strong tendency towards high Power Distance and to high Uncertainty Avoidance; in both cases there is a sharp contrast between the French and the Americans/British. This cultural profile is supposed to result in an attitude to authority which is relatively distant and unquestioning. Few people would deny that in general there is less discussion and more dictation which occurs in France between any boss and any subordinate. This might be given as a reason for believing that it would be impossible to implement a Reverse Appraisal scheme (a system which gives subordinates the opportunity to evaluate the performance of their boss) in France. The thinking would go something like this:

Since Reverse Appraisal implies discussion with and criticism of one's boss and since this represents a way of working and of interacting which is completely foreign to the majority in France, and since it is foreign to them because of the cultural make-up of the French, it would not work.

My reasoning would be different:

In France it is customary for bosses to maintain a distance between themselves and their team/ subordinates, it is not customary for the team to question the decisions of their boss. The introduction of a Reverse Appraisal scheme would necessitate a change in this fundamental relationship. That change would probably not be easy to effect. How easy or difficult it would be will depend entirely on the individuals concerned and their will to change. The decision to go ahead and try to implement such a scheme in France should be based on an intimate knowledge of the individuals concerned and the importance to the company of the change. The fact that Reverse Appraisal has been introduced successfully in one country should not be considered sufficient reason for attempting it elsewhere. The fact that the French are supposed to be high PD/UA should not be considered sufficient reason for not attempting it.

Whatever the prevalent cultural characteristics in a country may be, each country has large numbers of people who do not correspond to the rather tenuous norm. Consequently, in most countries deviation from this norm, even quite extreme deviation, will be acceptable. At the same time, most countries also have quite a strong sense of their own identity, be it cultural, familial, tribal, or whatever, and from this sense of identity comes a feeling of solidarity which results in the Germans being more German in a group when confronted with a Dutch group, the Spanish being more Spanish in a group when confronted with a Swedish ~roup. Both of these facts can be true simultaneously since most groups, national or otherwise, expect a certain level of conformism in terms of behaviour. In most groups this is a tacit and almost subconscious expectation; in some it is almost a presence. The fact that most groups conform to their past, and most individuals conform to their group's present means that knowing a little about how a group behaves in given situations is likely to be far more useful than knowing a lot about the average cultural profile.

Conformism is, in many ways, the most interesting dimension of culture and the one which is most neglected. Unlike the other elements of culture, conformism does truly appear to be a group phenomenon. While it is unusual to find very high levels of conformist expectation at country level, it seems to me to be very common to find high levels in smaller groups – families, companies, professions, sectors and so on. For a manager visiting an overseas company, having some indication of their conformist expectations is likely to be of much more use and, in any case, much more knowable, than their Power Distance index or their orientation in terms of the universalist/particularist continuum.

Japan is the obvious example of a country in which conformism is valued by the group, expected by the group and accorded by the individuals even when conformism means going along with something they do not believe in. However, even in this the Japanese only differ from other groups in terms of degree. Most of us would readily admit that there are times when we feel obliged to compromise on our behaviour, our feelings and our values in the interests of harmony – just another word for conformism. Whether we are trying to win a contract from another company, contributing to the smooth running of a project team or simply doing one's best to integrate in a new

'Did you say sheeps' eyes? Absolutely delicious!'

office, we are likely to subjugate some element of ourselves to what we perceive as being the norm. It is worth remembering this when we come up against what appears to be a solid wall of uniform difference – the wall may be made up of many bricks with which we are very familiar.

6 Active Compatibility

This chapter and those which follow it have as their objective to provide you the reader with strategies for increasing the chances of successful communication with individuals or groups whose culture is different from your own.

For communication to succeed a high level of compatibility is required. Compatibility can be considered in relation to a number of different factors. At the simplest level there needs to be compatibility of language – if the words that we use have one meaning to us and a different meaning to others, communication will not happen. Compatibility of values and beliefs is just as important but a little more complicated in that different values and beliefs can be compatible in spite of being different. Compatibility of behaviour is important too because any incompatibility is likely to have a negative effect on the goodwill of the parties to communication – goodwill being a very necessary ingredient of communication, even if it is not a sufficient ingredient.

It is very easy to say: 'We two are different and therefore incompatible, we cannot expect to be able to communicate, we can only do our best to manage without communication'. I believe it is also very common for the different parties to believe this, or at least to behave as if there were no way of overcoming essential differences or areas of incompatibility. This chapter aims to enumerate some of the things which can be done to achieve compatibility in terms of behaviour and also values and beliefs. I use the term 'active compatibility' to describe behaviour and processes which are intended to minimize areas of incompatibility.

The first step is to know who you are. The process of self-analysis described in Chapter 4 is vital for two reasons: Compatibility can only be achieved if you know what the two sides are. In order to accept that your values and beliefs are not universally held, that your behaviour is not the only one possible, you first have to know what your values and beliefs are and what your behaviour is.

The second step is knowing how your counterpart is different. In the case of values and beliefs, this is usually rather difficult. People do not walk around with labels on them saying: 'My fundamental beliefs are ... '. We may have to guess at them, basing our guesses on things they do or have done, things that they say or have said. We also need to understand the nature of possible differences. As I said earlier, the more strongly you believe something to be true, the more difficult it is to accept that someone else does not believe it, and the more difficult it is to accept that their point of view is just as valid as yours.

Here, the process of establishing what an opposite belief to your own might be is clearly fundamental to this process and it requires careful thought. Earlier I used the example of Honesty; another striking example could relate to killing. If you believe that *killing people is always wrong*, the opposite belief should be *killing people is not always wrong* – not *killing people is always right*. If you believe that *the prosperity of the company is more important than the quality of life of its employees*, the opposite belief is likely to be *the prosperity of the company depends on the quality of life of its employees*.

Active compatibility, in this context, means recognizing that there is some merit in the other belief, and that it is simply at the other end of a continuum, which begins with one belief and ends with another. Since you already know how you normally perceive the opposite belief, it is usually helpful to consider how someone with the opposite belief would perceive your position.

Take the example of the person who says: 'If my friend hits a pedestrian while driving above the speed limit and the pedestrian only suffers minor discomfort, I would feel able to lie on my friend's behalf and give evidence that he was driving within the speed limit. If on the other hand the pedestrian was seriously injured or killed, I would feel obliged to tell the truth'.

The person who believes the opposite would say: 'You mean that the worse the situation your friend found himself in, the less you would be inclined to help him?' Presented this way, your belief, eminently reasonable though it seemed to you, appears rather absurd.

Of course the particularist, who feels that his or her obligation to truth and justice grows in direct proportion to the seriousness of the consequences of his or her friend's actions, is unlikely to change that attitude, but they would do well to look at things from the other side, once in a while, even if it is just from another particularist angle. They may not be happy with the comparison but their story is not dissimilar to the one about the multi-millionaire who approached a woman and said:

'Would you sleep with me for a million pounds?'

On getting a positive response – if not necessarily an enthusiastic one – he said:

'Would you sleep with me for fifty pounds?'

Outraged, the woman replied:

'What do you think I am, a prostitute?'

'We have already established that,' said the man, 'we're just negotiating the price!'

Another example of the way in which you can look at attitudes in two different ways is to consider a collectivist approach to life.

The collectivist might say of an individualist: 'You can't trust him, he won't even help his family and friends.' The individualist might simultaneously be saying: 'You can't trust him, he always promotes the interests of his family and friends.' Both assertions sound equally reasonable, but all of us would come down firmly on one side or the other, in any given situation, and almost always condemn the other point of view out of hand. Again, recognizing that there is merit in a different world view is a step towards compatibility.

Compatibility and complementarity

The old saying 'When in Rome do as Rome does' is perhaps the most obvious example of active compatibility. Too many expatriates do their best to recreate a micro version of the society from which they are in temporary exile and to lead a life which is unchanged. British holidaymakers are perhaps the worst, in that they colonize resorts in hotter climates and do their best to avoid any contact with the local culture, cuisine or people. To be fair, I can't think of many nationalities which show themselves off to good advantage when they are on holiday. In any case, compatibility does not mean changing one's culture or personality – 'going native' as certain expansionist groups would have called it dismissively – it simply means looking for what is good in another and enjoying it. Indeed, it would be a mistake to be disloyal to one's own culture or pretend to be. As long ago as the first century AD Juvenal remarked of the Greek tutors which were fashionable in chic Roman households at the time: 'When you smile they laugh, when you look sad they shed tears and when you say I'm hot, they begin to perspire.' He was not complimenting them on their active compatibility, rather he was criticizing them for dissimulation. Any individual who has any national pride expects others to have national pride too, and s/he will not respect someone who seems to shed their nationality or their culture as they move around the world. Even the self-deprecation which is common among certain groups in Britain and elsewhere can affect the way that the individual is perceived, though it will not change perceptions of their nation.

Some elements of individual culture seem so deep-rooted as to be genetic. Whether they are or not does not really matter, the fact that they are never questioned, does. Attitudes to time, which have been discussed before, are one such example. If you are the monochronic type who believes that a meeting scheduled at 10.00a.m. should begin at 10.00a.m. sharp and that anyone arriving after that time is late, rude, unprofessional, incompetent and a host of other negative things, you probably have never thought that they may not consider themselves to be late. What?! you say, how can they deny their lateness? It's a matter of fact not opinion. However, it may be that your counterpart, be s/he from overseas or not, has a different perception. In the case of meetings of a group or a team, attendance at the 10.00a.m. meeting can be seen as: *being present at some point in a meeting which may or may not begin at 10.00a.m.* To this counterpart, 10.00a.m. may be a guideline, it may be an ideal, even if it is an official start-time it will have a certain tolerance built into it. The person who perceives things in this way is quite likely to annoy you further by holding side conversations during the meeting, using the mobile phone or leaving the meeting to take messages, even leaving the meeting altogether before it has finished. You may believe that there is no way that this person can be effective, but you have no evidence to support your theory; quite the opposite in fact. In any case how many times have you dreamt of being the kind of person who happily has three telephone conversations at the same time, shouting 'Buy' into one, 'Sell' into another and 'Shall we say dinner at Quaglino's?' into a third! If this person has noticed that you are always on time, s/he may even think less of you as a result. Haven't you got anything else to do, other than to attend meetings? If this counterpart of yours is on his/her way to the monthly briefing and bumps into a colleague or client that s/he has not seen for sometime, s/he will stop and chat. That is how the polychronic person prefers to communicate, through informal discussions, personal networks and so on. However annoying it may be for you that s/he seems better informed than you, after attending less than half the meeting/s, you have to recognize that it can be effective. On the exceptional occasion when you arrive late, or after your polychronic counterpart, you don't find him/her tapping feet, looking at the clock and muttering about your nationality; s/he has got the briefcase out, notebook computer on, or mobile phone steaming, and ridiculous though it may seem, s/he seems less stressed than you.

Compatibility means recognizing that your counterpart's is a valid way of behaving – and maybe learning something from it. You will not become polychronic, but you may have something to do while you wait for him/her in future. As I said above, difference does not preclude compatibility. What you are looking for when you have recognized the validity of a different way of looking at things, is complementarity. The monochronic and polychronic types can be members of a very successful team together. Every strength implies a weakness and vice versa, and only by combining different types can you achieve a really substantial whole. The key words which combine to make complementarity a possibility are *Responsibility* and *Respect*. Respect for different points of view, respect for different behaviours, respect for the person who is rarely seen after 6.00p.m. because they value their home life, respect for the person who can tell a joke in the pub after work but who appears to be humourless at work – since they do not see humour as playing a role in professional life.

Responsibility is hard work

Responsibility is perhaps more like hard work. By responsibility I mean taking 100% responsibility for communication. Given how difficult it can be to communicate successfully, it is very important that each party should make the maximum effort. However, since we cannot assume that all parties approach a communication event with the same commitment, goodwill and so on, those who *are* committed need to think always in terms of the sending and the receiving of the message. Too many people satisfy themselves with sending or receiving. The attitude of the person who says: 'I sent the message; it's not my fault if it was not received', reveals that they are missing a very important point. There is no merit in sending a message if it is sent on the wrong wavelength. Taking responsibility means making sure, as far as possible, that messages arrive. This will often mean finding out whether the receiver is tuned to the same wavelength and if necessary resending on a new wavelength. You may even discover that the receiver is turned off, in which case you have to find out why – and of course how to turn it on; metaphorically speaking. When receiving, responsibility means making sure that your receiver is switched on and then tuning and retuning until you are receiving loud and clear.

All too often I have heard people say: 'I'm not going to cooperate because I wasn't consulted', or because the decision was communicated clumsily. If this is the case, action has to be taken – the last thing you want is to get yourself, or your team, a reputation for being uncooperative. Taking responsibility means making sure that there is every reason for including you/your team in decision-making. Another example of the negative attitude I am describing is that of the person who goes to presentations or training events with 'Convince me' written all over his/her face, or even 'Entertain me'. Bearing in mind that the vast majority of presentations, and all training events are in-house activities designed or intended to develop or inform the participants, we ought to be thinking of ways of making the presenter/trainer's job easier, not more difficult. When the presenter is of a different nationality/cultural background to the majority of the audience this becomes all the more important.

Another side to responsibility requires every individual to identify areas of incompatibility which stem from different practices. Different ways of doing business, of approaching clients, of running meetings, of communicating may be just as incompatible as different ways of accounting. Ignoring these differences will most definitely not make them go away. On the other hand, there are probably areas of compatibility and common ground which are not being exploited. When you are looking for ways of reconciling the irreconcilable it pays to *accentuate the positive*. You will find that while the methods are incompatible, the objectives and the needs are the same – while the procedures are at odds, the logic underlying them may be the same – although there may have been two different points of departure. When engineers are working with engineers, accountants with accountants, HR people with HR people, there will be enormous tracts of common ground on which to build new, compatible ways of working and working together.

Many people have an instinct for finding the common ground which they share with colleagues, clients and new acquaintances. In the UK when people meet for the first time, they very often go through an elaborate questioning procedure designed precisely to establish what, if anything, they have in common with the new person. Different people in different countries have different

approaches, different taboo subjects; the goal remains the same – to establish reasons for communicating, above and beyond what is simply polite and civilized.

A friend of mine was overseeing the acquisition of a British company by a French company. A number of French managers had been moved into positions in the UK but a certain amount of friction was apparent. On one particular day my friend was approached independently by one of the British managers and one of the French managers. The French manager said:

'I don't understand the British; I hardly know these people and yet they keep asking me really personal questions, about my family and what I do at the weekend and so on!'

The British manager said:

'It's getting me down working with the French; they talk about nothing but work, they never want to know anything about me, they're not interested in me as a person!'

The fact that they both approached my friend on the same day was a coincidence. The fact that they both felt able to approach him was a tribute to his ability to relate to both groups. He was then able to explain that although they each had the desire to build a relationship, they had different ways of going about it. A little mutual awareness can go a long way. What appears to be difference may turn out to be different sides of the same coin.

7 International English

The world of business is shrinking fast. It is now commonplace for managers to travel overseas on short trips and extended assignments. Getting there is easy, how to communicate once you arrive, however, presents many managers with difficulties.

When you have to liaise with Germany one day, France the next and Japan the day after, learning the relevant foreign languages is clearly not practical for most people. Even if you most often have contact with one particular country, it is quite likely that you have neither the time nor the budget necessary to permit you to master the language. So you speak in English – but do you communicate?

The phrase: 'They all speak English there' which we constantly hear, is not only very rarely true, it also begs the question: 'How well do they speak English?' The level of English at which a person can survive a one-to-one conversation with a colleague on a known subject is very different from the level necessary to follow a complex presentation, training session or conference.

Even meetings can present very real difficulties to non-native speakers; they spend so much time understanding what has been said, that they have no time to formulate their own contribution, even assuming that they would dare to contribute in their faltering English.

It is very easy to assume that silence indicates agreement, that 'no questions' implies understanding and assent. Afterwards, when the customer does not buy, when no action follows the meeting, when the training session bears no fruit and when the project team continues to be at crossed purposes, the presenter will blame everyone except him/herself.

Years of experience, courses in Presentation Skills and the best will in the world will not compensate for the fact that your audience did not go to school in English, you are not speaking their language.

Clearly a number of questions need to be asked about how we go about communicating in English, for most people would accept that answers very rarely appear without questions being asked. The aim of this short chapter is to pose some of the questions (and suggest possible answers) and further, to encourage the reader to ask him/herself the right questions, without which the answers will not be forthcoming. Some of the guidelines given apply equally to communication which does not cross national frontiers.

There is only one language in which to communicate to a multinational audience: International English. There are different versions of it and different definitions. At Business Expression we define it as:

A low-risk language appropriate for audiences whose mother-tongue is not English.

A bit of a mouthful, I know, because it is a catch-all definition and it is intended to be. Our starting point is the belief that there is little point in inventing a new language which needs to be learned when we can adapt one that we already know. There are no hard-and-fast rules about how and what to adapt, only guidelines. First we should clarify what is meant by 'low-risk language'.

Words, phrases and structures which are in little danger of being misunderstood.

Vocabulary

Many of those who have attended seminars on this subject have said that International English is just simple English:

' . . . in other words the kind of language you would use to a child, words of one syllable.'

Using this definition of simple English we compiled the following list of examples of words which every child knows and which could hardly be shorter:

GET	PUT
get up	put up
get down	put down
get over	put over
get out	put out
get about	put about
get away	put away
get away with	put up with
get on	put on
get by	put by
get off	put off
get down to	put down to
get up to	put up to

Simple English?

There are two good reasons why these are not examples of low-risk English:

1 They are idiomatic verbs not learned in schools overseas (with some exceptions).

2 They are very short words, often swallowed by the speaker and therefore not easily heard.

If you were to *write* a speech or a presentation, you would probably find that you used fewer of the idiomatic verbs mentioned above. Only the most assiduous students of Sir Ernest Gowers' *The Complete Plain Words* actively avoid words with a Latin or Greek root. Consequently your speech would contain *possibles* instead of *cans*; *obligations* instead of *musts*; *escape* instead of *get away*; and *tolerate* instead of *put up with*.

If we consider which words are most likely to be understood by non-English members of the audience, it would not be contentious to assume that the Latinate words are a better bet. Nor is it only the continental Europeans who are likely to favour these words. The greatest weakness of the Japanese and those from the far East/South East Asia in general, lies in their listening comprehension; a longer word requiring a more deliberate delivery is therefore much more likely to be understood by your average Japanese listener.

The simple guideline, in terms of vocabulary, is to prefer the Latin word to the Saxon. Of course this advice should not be taken to extremes. If you choose words of Latin or Greek origin which would challenge a native-speaker of English with an average level of education, then you are going too far. I would not suggest for a moment that:

Expectoration is prohibited was preferable to *No spitting*.

Idioms

Different people have, quite naturally, different tendencies when it comes to expressing themselves. Jargon, which is effectively a form of idiom, has a habit of inventing itself in every occupation – professional or other.

Jargon in itself is not necessarily a bad thing. Inventing a word to fulfil a very specific function can aid communication, particularly within a given occupation. The criticisms levelled at jargon are principally two:

1 In many cases a new word is superfluous since an existing word could fulfil the function without leading to confusion.

2 Not everybody will understand the jargon, particularly if they come from a different country as well as a different occupation.

I recently heard a Quality Engineer tell his wife that the position in which she had parked her car was suboptimal. In my opinion his choice of words, like his wife's parking, was suboptimal, but I should think that on this occasion the message got through.

In other cases communication is definitely at risk and it is certainly worth remembering the computer expression GIGO (Garbage In Garbage Out) since it applies just as much to communication.

Since both the British and the Americans are very keen on sport, many examples of sporting jargon have crept into everyday language - everyday, that is, if you are British or American – but can you expect your French and German counterparts to understand the following:

A Good Sport

a sticky wicket
a straight bat
a good innings
an own goal
snookered

kick into touch
plain sailing
neck and neck
below the belt
behind the 8-ball
a different ball-park
sitting in the catbird seat

Even if you are not an inveterate sportsman, you may well be one of those who feel that they are going to seem very boring if they do not pepper their language with idioms or colourful phrases of one kind or another. There are metaphors which are more or less transparent and which can be just as colourful as idioms. A certain amount of attention is necessary since there are those who cannot think of a metaphor without mixing it; and you can understand how a non-native speaker of English might be a little surprised to hear, as I did not long ago, that skating on thin ice can land you in hot water!

It is easy to forgive the Frenchman who assumes that Euro-Disney is an example of a Mickey Mouse operation; and how many times have you used the following in conversation:

Idiomania
A shot in the dark
It's your funeral
They missed the boat
A needle in a haystack
Make ends meet
Go by the book
Hit the nail on the head
Flog a dead horse
Take the mickey
Keep on your toes
Rock the boat

'So, if this customer was just the tip of the iceberg, why are they not pleased that we missed the boat?'

Tip of the iceberg
Red herring
White elephant
Water under the bridge
He's two sandwiches short of a picnic
Run it up the flagpole and see who salutes it

Overqualification

It is often a useful exercise when writing a report or even a letter to reread the finished document and remove the words which add nothing to the sense. If you heard a tape of an average meeting or conversation, the same exercise would reveal far more superfluous words and even phrases.

Often the superfluous words have been put in to embellish, sometimes to qualify, and often just to fill in potential gaps caused by hesitation. In other cases it is quite beyond me to explain why certain words constantly creep into conversations.

For the non-native listener these words constitute interference. They add little or nothing to the meaning and yet they need to be heard and understood before they can be dismissed.

Since they have such minimal importance they are often spoken very quickly or swallowed – a subconscious recognition of the fact that they are not useful. This means that they are that much more difficult to understand; furthermore, if it is not clear to the listener what function a particular word or phrase fulfils they are more likely to assume that they are missing something.

The following list contains some words/phrases used to qualify, and others which are simply difficult to understand:

Sorta
Kinda
Helluva
Bitova
Like (as in: it's like difficult to ...)

Amazingly
Incredibly
Pretty

So to speak
As such
In a manner of speaking
In (actual) fact
Actually

You know
D'you see

Know what I mean?

Whatchamacallit
Thingummyjig
Doobry

When you are analysing your speech patterns and noting the recurrence of certain words and phrases you need to ask yourself one simple question:

Does this word or phrase add anything or contribute to making my point clearly?

If the answer is *No*, if it does not add anything to the meaning, it probably takes something away from the communication.

The long and the short of it

'I met this guy the other day on an NLP course, an ex-banker, bit of a BOBO, drives a Jag, anyway he's just landed himself a job with NATO ....'

Many abbreviations and acronyms have found their way into conversational English and are so well established that we assume everybody understands them. However, when you consider that the French for NATO is OTAN and that NLP is PNL, the United Nations is ONU and God alone knows what BOBO is in French (burnt out but opulent) you will not be very surprised when I tell you that such terms are going to have a very uncommunicative effect.

Within a given company it is quite possible that acronyms do form part of the company language; it should never be assumed to be the case, and even when you know it to be the case, there may be differences in the way an acronym is pronounced, e.g. ISO 9000. Now you know, all you have to do is remember.

ACROMNEMONIC

A	C	R	O	N	Y	M	S
B	A	E	B	I	U	A	H
B	N	N	S	M	P	Y	O
R		D	C	B	P		C
E		E	U	Y	I		K
V		R	R		E		
I			E	a			
A				n			
T				d			
I							
O							
N							

There are of course situations in which TLAs and FLAs are acceptable, even preferable. They may encourage a feeling of being part of an in-group provided everyone does know what they mean. A glossary in a hand-out may be the way to ensure that this is the case.

Oh, by the way, TLA means Three Letter Acronym and of course an FLA has Four Letters!

Say what you mean

In spite of the heading this section refers mainly to written language although there are principles which apply just as well to the spoken word. Standard English and particularly British English is a language which loves euphemisms and understatement. The effects on the success of communication are

Approximate English	**Meaning in Standard English**
Actions	shares in a company
Actual/actually	current/at the moment
Agenda	diary
Assist	attend (a conference, meeting)
Benefit	profit
Claim	to complain
Conception	design
Competence/concurrence	competition
Conference	lecture
Control	to check
Convenient	reasonable, fair (of prices)
Delay	lead time/delivery
Demand	to ask for
Design	to draw
Dismiss	to resign
Employee	worker (as opposed to manager)
Eventually	potentially, perhaps, if the case arises
Exercise	financial year
Formation	Training
Funny	enjoyable
Furnish, furniture	to supply/supplies
Gentleman	Sir (like 'Gentlemen' but used in the singular)
Hardly	hard (e.g. work) or with difficulty
Important	big
Interesting	profitable
Invite	I invite you = it's my treat/it's

	on me
Meaning	opinion
My Dear	old chap, my friend
Offer	supply (as in supply and demand)
Particular	individual, strange
Piece	unit or (spare) part
Pretend	to claim
Problem	matter or issue (not always negative in Approximate English)
Resume	to sum up
Rentability	profitability
Security	safety
Society	a company
Sympathetic	nice (of a person or place)
Used to	I usually ...
With pleasure	Yes, please

When a person is making the supreme sacrifice of communicating with you in your language rather than their own, it is extremely frustrating for them to see your look of incomprehension when they 'slightly' mispronounce a word, use a phrase which is perhaps a direct translation, or choose a term which is not strictly speaking the *mot juste*. If you consciously acknowledge that you are using International English and constantly remind yourself that what you will hear is not always going to be Standard English, you stand a better chance of understanding the variants which are to be found in Approximate English. You need to pay closer attention to the context in which a conversation or presentation is placed and adopt active listening techniques which may include periodic – but not too frequent – paraphrases of what has been said. At the same time you need to attempt to follow the logic of what is being said rather than simply the words. After all, a short word like *not* can easily be omitted by someone speaking English as a foreign language; if you are taking everything at face value, you may conclude that the speaker is somewhat muddled in his/her thinking. Remember the concept of responsibility in communication and remember that by speaking your language your interlocutor is probably suffering agonies at not being able to express themselves as fluently and as clearly as they would in their own language.

Above all, never fall into the all too common trap of believing that your counterpart is of low intelligence, simply because he or she finds it difficult to communicate clearly in *your* language.

8 International Meetings

They say that 50% of money spent on advertising is wasted and that the difficulty lies in determining which 50%. A similar comment could be made about meetings: 50% of time spent in meetings is wasted, but which 50%? If seems likely that the percentage is even higher in the case of international meetings. Wouldn't it be nice therefore, if this chapter could be called *How to behave (always) in international meetings*? Unfortunately, with meetings – as with everything else – there is no universal answer. In any case it is not very helpful to know how meetings between people of different nationalities should be run if you are never in a position to dictate the *modus operandi*. However, any participant in a meeting has the opportunity of influencing how future meetings will be run, if s/he can find ways of behaving, ways of proceeding which are acceptable to all and which do not demand too much change of any one participant or group of participants.

Quite apart from the different behaviours which can be encountered in meetings, the differing expectations of those present create problems. Inevitably a meeting which does not correspond to the expectations of the participants has a destabilizing effect. One of the comments which I have most often heard on this subject, goes like this:

'I come to the meeting fully prepared to discuss the subject/s in question and to help to contribute to the

'Lunch is for losers, Jacques, let's send out for a couple of Big Macs.'

decision. When I get to the meeting I discover that the decision has already been made and that the meeting is a long-winded way of communicating the decision to the unconsulted masses.'

I have heard English people say this about French companies, French about German companies and Germans say it about British companies. In my experience it usually happens when head office is meeting with a subsidiary or a division, although you can be sure that the French, Germans or British will be blamed, on the basis that it forms part of their incomprehensible business culture.

There are so many variables in meetings, international or otherwise, from the way the decision to have a meeting is made and communicated, and the information in terms of agendas and other materials which go out (or do not) before the meeting, to the management of the meeting (if and how) and the extent to which an agenda is respected or even acknowledged; Who is at the meeting and how much they contribute also varies a great deal from company to company, and from country to country. In some companies there is a strict and, in my opinion, a wise policy of discouraging attendance from those who could not, if asked, clearly explain why they are attending, in terms of what they can contribute to the meeting. In some countries, however, the status of an individual will be judged and demonstrated by the number of assistants, sidekicks or subordinates which they bring with them. In some cases these supernumeraries will not contribute at all, other than through their boss, i.e. when s/he has a whispered conversation with them before speaking.

Beyond advising on the fact that in nearly every case there are some norms which are recognized and conformed to, and that as a visitor one is best advised to try to divine these norms and adhere to them, I think it would be best if I limited my comments to meetings which take place within a given company or group of companies, between people whose levels, if not equal, are at least comparable and who are meeting as a team.

Transparency

If the main source of problems in meetings is a discrepancy between one set of expectations and another or others, the second source is almost certainly different procedures, both in terms of the communication which surrounds the meeting and which takes place in it, and also in terms of the way of proceeding towards an agreed goal and making a decision, if that is the objective of the meeting.

Very often, cross-cultural encounters resemble nothing so much as a game of chess. In chess, each player has his/her own game plan. The game plan of each is unknown to the other and each may think at some stage that they recognize the game plan of the other and may be proved wrong at a later stage. In chess it is rather important that one's game plan should not be revealed to the counterpart, because it is a competitive situation and is meant to be. In cross-cultural encounters the players very often go through the same process of trying to guess, based on what they see and hear, the game plan of the others; in other words, by listening and watching one tries to establish where one's counterpart is coming from and where they are going to. The difference is that in the cross-cultural communication there is not (generally) supposed to be a competitive element. So why should we have to guess and hint? Why do we not ask and tell?

Transparency, by which I mean the habit of making your position perfectly clear and asking your counterpart to do the same, will very often be the way forward. By talking about the differences between you openly, you can achieve the same effect as turning on a light in a darkened room. Instead of stumbling around in darkness, you can proceed with confidence, with the additional comfort of knowing that you have started to build a relationship of which the foundations are laid on trust.

The mutual awareness which should result from a policy of transparency is likely to be beneficial in other situations too. As far as the meetings are concerned, it may result in the establishment of procedures which are new to both/all parties but which are designed to recognize the different starting points of each and to meet an agreed set of objectives. The agreed procedure is also very likely to reduce the stress which for many people is inherent in a situation of uncertainty and vagueness.

Without wanting to anticipate the results of such frank and open exchanges, it may very well happen that transparency reveals that one individual or group is accustomed to making decisions on the basis of a majority, irrespective of the strength of feeling of the minority, while another group or individual is in the habit of rejecting simple majority rule, in favour of achieving consensus even if it takes much longer. A difference of this kind will not necessarily be solved simply by being revealed, but it is certainly a difference which needs to be highlighted and which needs to be discussed.

There is another way in which communication in meetings and elsewhere can lack transparency. E.T. Hall, who was mentioned earlier, divides communication styles into two distinct tendencies: High Context and Low Context. Very briefly, these two opposing tendencies can be defined as follows:

High context communication depends heavily on the implicit, the unspoken; in other words a great deal is taken for granted. Those who communicate in this way read and 'write' between the lines.

Low context communication depends on the explicit, indeed there is nothing which is implicit; if it is not said it is not communicated.

Hall believes that certain countries display strong tendencies towards one style or the other. In truth, most in-groups will, to a greater or lesser extent, indulge in high context communication. Manifestations of high context communication are: jargon, unfinished sentences, winks, knowing smiles, etc. Successful high context communication depends on an extensive shared experience, shared values and beliefs and so on. The outsider will often be mystified, having the impression that s/he understands the words which are being said without having any idea of what is really going on. In International meetings, attempts at high context communication are usually doomed to failure or worse. Low context communication, where nothing is assumed and everything which is to be communicated is spoken in unambiguous terms, is a much surer way of avoiding misunderstanding, even though it may appear to be blunt, undiplomatic and even rude at times. Self-awareness is crucial in these circumstances because there is not usually a conscious decision to communicate in one way or the other. The responsibility will generally fall on the outsider to make it clear when s/he is not receiving the message. Unfortunately the outsider is often reluctant to admit that they do not understand what is going on, for fear of underlining the fact that they do not belong to the in-group.

A colleague of mine recently attended an international training session organized by the UK head office of a large consultancy group. With the exception of the facilitators, none of the delegates was a native speaker of English. In the joining instructions delegates were informed that the dress code for the event was 'smart but casual'. My colleague was asked by a group of delegates, on the evening before the training was to start, what was meant by this and a lively discussion ensued which involved most of those present, none of whom could confidently say that s/he would be appropriately dressed when the seminar began.

The UK training administrator undoubtedly thought that he was being helpful by including this 'information' in the instructions, but he may as well have written it in ancient Icelandic for all the help it gave. If the delegates had looked up the words 'smart' and 'casual' in the dictionary they might have found 'neat' but 'informal' as alternatives. Bearing in mind that concepts of both neatness and informality are likely to vary from place to place and group to group, they might still have made wrong decisions. Furthermore, the dictionary which would have told them that the expression is generally interpreted by those who are familiar with it as meaning 'no ties, no jeans' has yet to be written.

In certain situations where groups or teams made up of different nationalities will have to work together and meet regularly for a period of time, it may be desirable to use a facilitator to oversee meetings, at least during the early stages of a project. In some companies, rather than involve someone from outside the team for any length of time, groups have opted for a revolving chairperson role to ensure that ground rules which have been established at the beginning are adhered to. Differing attitudes to rules mean that success is not guaranteed in this way, indeed individuals can become frustrated by a rather relaxed approach to rules displayed by people who have contributed to the definition of the rules. The use of a facilitator to 'police' meetings can help by focusing frustration, if there is to be any, on a person who is not of the team; furthermore, once a routine has been established, teams will readily pursue it even after any kind of enforcement is removed.

9 International Presentations

Many of the guidelines which are essential to International Presentations (i.e. presentations to audiences which include non-native speakers of English) apply also to presentations to native speakers. I shall concentrate here on those points which are especially important when addressing non-natives, and on any points which differ from a universal best practice.

It is worth remembering that any form of oral communication is a kind of presentation. It is therefore true that in meetings and even in conversation many of the guidelines should be followed.

Structure and planning

It has already been observed that when *writing* a speech or presentation the language which flows naturally from your pen is more likely to be appropriate to an international audience than your everyday way of speaking would be. It follows therefore that writing your presentation is a positive first step. The second step would be learning the content and key phrases of your talk. The reason for this is that whereas a written talk is often a good talk, a talk which is read is always a bad one. When reading, you will speak more quickly (assuming that you can read your writing), you will face your audience less, and your intonation will go out of the window.

However, you should not get into the situation where if you depart from your script or forget the exact wording, you dry up or look around for the prompt. This is why I say learn the *content* and the *key phrases*.

Many well-prepared presenters let themselves down as soon as there is a question or interruption by departing from their prepared script and reverting to everyday language. For this reason the preparation of a clear response to anticipated questions is to be recommended. Remember that even if a question is posed by a native speaker, the whole audience should understand your response. (See also the section on Q&A, pages 104–6.)

Having decided that you are going to write your piece, you have to define the structure. Perhaps the oldest and still the best advice to follow is what a colleague of mine calls the Sergeant Major's Advice:

Tell them what you are going to tell them.
Tell them.
Tell them what you have told them.

Why? Because it prepares them for what they are going to hear and provides a few landmarks, it gives them the chance to catch what they missed, and it gives you a chance to communicate your key messages at least three times. Add to this a preamble which will get them on your side (see below) and a conclusion which thanks them and encourages questions – and there is your structure. The saying *If you fail to prepare, be prepared to fail* is never more appropriate than in the context of an international presentation.

Signposts

Having established a transparent structure for your presentation, you will need to appreciate that a momentary lapse in the concentration of your audience, or a few words missed for lack of vocabulary, can have dramatic effects on your audience's overall understanding. Whereas the native can dream about the new girl/boy in the accounts department for five minutes and still gather the essentials of what you have to say, the non-native finds it much more difficult to follow when the sequence of ideas is interrupted.

Anybody who has ever learned a foreign language will tell you that the phrase which is most difficult to understand is the phrase without context. If somebody comes up to you in a hotel lounge, somebody you have never met before, and speaks, even the person with a good level in the language is likely to ask them to repeat themselves.

For the same reason, the non-native member of the audience

cannot afford to relax his/her concentration, thereby losing the sense of context; nonetheless it does happen; what you have to do therefore is to make it easy for the person to get back into the swing. You do this by providing signposts – words or phrases which are periodically (and quite often) uttered, indicating where you have been, where you are and where you are going – in terms of your presentation of course.

Example: *I have said enough about the technical benefits of the product, now I would like to tell you about the price;*

or: *That concludes point one, Quality. Before moving on to consider point two, permit me to explain the* ....

Delivery and pace

Anybody who has learned German will tell you of the frustration which they felt, at first, when waiting for the key word – the verb – which is so often placed at the end of the sentence.

Non-native speakers of English often feel a similar frustration when waiting for the speaker who has elected to speak – very – slowly – to – his – non – native – audience.

Understanding usually implies the recognition of phrases, not individual words. If you deliver the words very slowly, the listener, be s/he native or not, is invited constantly to guess what the subsequent words are going to be. If s/he guesses wrongly, as is most often the case, with every new word s/he has to reconsider the whole phrase, the beginning of which may have been a long time ago.

I
I shall
I shall put
I shall put up

I shall put up with
I shall put up with this
I shall put up with this no
I shall put up with this no longer

This represents the difficulty presented by slow deliberate delivery.

It is easier for all concerned if you speak at a gentle, near normal pace, enunciating clearly and allowing a pause between ideas, rather than between words. One of the advantages of a properly prepared presentation is that you are in a position to impose a rigorous logic on your presentation, which will make it possible to avoid constant parentheses, provisos and phrases beginning with: 'Having said that ... ' In any case, I would boldly suggest that nine out of ten such provisos are superfluous.

On your side

It is truly a shame that, even when presenting to people from your own company, it should be necessary to win them over, to persuade them to listen to you and be patient with you if anything goes wrong.

Too little is said about the responsibility of audiences to help presenters. However, I have already raised the subject in this book and we can only hope that, in the future, as much attention will be paid to audience skills training as is currently paid to presentation skills training. Enough said.

So how should you go about getting your non-natives on your side? Most presenters seem to think that humour is an essential part of any presentation, that without humour your audience is going to turn off immediately and not switch back on. The presenter who begins 'A funny thing happened on my way here today' or 'Did you hear the one about . . . ' may be on the point of telling a very amusing anecdote. However, his non-native audience is already lost because they do not recognize that he is about to tell a joke.

Suppose for a moment that something about the presenter's demeanour lets them know that a joke is coming. What are the chances of them understanding the joke? If they understand it – and we are getting into the realms of the very unlikely here – how sure can we be that they will all find it funny? Finally if we stretch this hypothesis to the limit and say that this particular group considers it to be a funny joke – will they consider it appropriate? We have to bear in mind that in some countries humour and business are considered to be incompatible.

If you are prepared to depend on all these IFs being fulfilled simultaneously, then by all means start with a joke. If you are not such a gambler, it is worth taking into account that this obsession with humour is far from being universal and it follows therefore that there are other ways of securing the goodwill of your audience. The easiest ways, I suggest, include the following:

- The French have a saying, *Souriez, on vous repondra*. Smile and people will smile back.

- Say a few words in the appropriate language/s and apologize for not presenting in their language/s.

- Show that you know something (good) about their country/ies.

- Talk to *them*, not to the flipchart/OHP/screen.

- Thank them for being there.

- Show that you have prepared yourself – no other compliment is as sincere.

I heard of a man who was addressing a group of Japanese business people; he began:

'There was an Englishman, a Frenchman and a German . . .'

If I were an American I would begin by telling you a joke.
If I were Japanese I would probably begin with an apology.

Since I am neither American nor Japanese, let me begin by apologizing for not telling a joke.

It shows preparation, knowledge of the prevailing traditions, and satisfied his own need for a light-hearted introduction – just right.

Visual aids

You know as well as I do that visual aids very rarely aid. Large wodges of text bunged onto a transparency, indecipherable hieroglyphics scrawled onto flipcharts and complex graphics flashed up, talked over, and removed, cannot be seen as helping.

Before preparing or using any visual aid ask yourself:

What purpose is it going to serve?

In precisely what way is it going to help?

If you cannot answer these questions satisfactorily, both before and after (in the case of aids which you are preparing) then you are not aiding.

A text on a transparency is never an aid, not least because the average presenter cannot stop him/herself from speaking over it, nor does s/he leave it up for long enough.

If you are tempted to put a text on a transparency it is almost certainly something which should be distributed before the meeting or presentation, and certainly something which should be available for taking away afterwards.

Visual aids, genuine ones, are usually *prepared* transparencies which illustrate something which is either difficult to explain orally, e.g. a spiral staircase, or which will have a greater impact when it is presented visually, e.g. a graph which contrasts the trends of a number of comparable companies.

Before showing a visual aid, explain what your audience is going to see and why. Present your visual aid and, if necessary, explain how it works. Then give your audience enough time to take it in – in silence. Finally, make sure that it has achieved its objective. This does not mean saying: *OK everybody?* and moving on.

The prepared visual aid is much more likely to be genuine than an attempt to bolster your presentation with flipchart scrawlings. We all know this and yet how often do we see presenters abandon their audiences by turning their backs to write, in semi-legible script, one or two words which contribute nothing.

'Today I'm going to talk to your about Quality' . . . Presenter scribbles *Quality* at an angle, on the flipchart. Why? What useful purpose does it serve? For the next ten minutes the presenter is competing with the flipchart for the attention of his audience who, amateur graphologists to a man, analyse his character, wonder why he has written this one word on the chart, or daydream about the shapes of the letters.

If you do not have a use for the flipchart, it is probably wiser to move, or indeed to remove it. The average presenter, and even some above-average presenters, apparently feel obliged to use the flipchart – just because it is there. I am not saying that it does not have a use; it will, for example, enable you to explain visually, difficulties which you had not predicted. It can be used to record contributions from the audience; but having achieved whatever it is that you are trying to achieve, turn the page. Do not create distractions for your audience. That is something which they can do for themselves.

If you have to use the flipchart (*paperboard* in Approximate English), it is important to remember that the handwriting of other nationalities is notoriously difficult to read, abbreviations (q.v.) are high-risk, and numbers need particular attention. Even today many people seem not to have registered the fact that, in many countries, the comma which for me and probably you indicates thousands, is replaced by a full-stop and the decimal point is replaced by a comma.

Checking understanding and Q & A

As mentioned above, the prevailing method of checking understanding, namely asking 'OK?' and moving on, is simply not good enough in the international environment; indeed, it is rarely good enough when language is not an issue. What then are the alternatives?

Checking understanding should be seen as an activity which is continuous, which carries on throughout your presentation, and which principally involves nothing more complicated than genuine eye-contact.

If I were to run a course on audience skills, one of the main themes which I would stress would be the need for audience members to provide feedback to the speaker, to enable him/her to gauge the audience's level of understanding and/or agreement. Most audiences are at best impassive and at worst inclined to give misleading signals. For the time being (i.e. until all audiences have been trained) it is the job of the presenter to read in the faces of the audience members when they have not understood, when they are not convinced, when they disagree violently, when they need further examples, when they are having difficulty relating what the speaker is saying to their own experience, and so on.

The question-and-answer session is another important way of checking your audience's understanding and reactions. For this reason it may be desirable to include Q & A at key points during your presentation, not just at the end. The difficulty here is that the average non-native speaker is a little reluctant to raise his/her hand and put questions in his/her faltering English, even supposing that they would normally be inclined to – bearing in mind that many *native* speakers are hesitant about asking questions in a group presentation.

You therefore need to make it easier for people to ask questions. One way would be to break down your presentation, or a section of it, into key points and ask if anyone would appreciate further explanation of point 1/2/3, etc. In this way the member of the audience only needs to nod or say 'Yes' at the relevant moment.

The Q & A session which follows your presentation is a little more tricky. Most people like to have questions asked, but they need to create a situation in which members of the audience feel comfortable.

Suggestion 1: Allow a pause during which the audience are asked to write their questions down. You then have the additional benefit of being able to deal with the questions in a logical order.

Suggestion 2: Divide your audience into subgroups, each with a spokesperson, to discuss what questions need to be asked/answered. You can either appoint a spokesperson yourself, or encourage each group to do so.

Suggestion 3: Tell your audience that if there are any questions, you will be happy to answer them, and that to this end you will be at the bar/in the lounge/at their disposal for the next hour.

The practice of repeating or reformulating the question is also advisable; as well as giving you the opportunity to think, it will ensure that you are answering the question that was put. It will also give you the opportunity to make a native speaker's question intelligible to the non-native speakers and, perhaps, vice versa. Don't forget that it is vital to take all questions and questioners seriously and a good idea to thank them for their question. If the question appears to be stupid, your immediate reaction should be that you have not understood it. If it really is a stupid question, rather than dismissing it, answer it and enlarge on it in such a way as to make it less obvious that the question was not really thought out.

Hand-outs

The subject of when – and even if – hand-outs should be given is one which presenters have agonized over since the Ten Commandments. In the case of presentations to non-native speakers, there is really no question as to whether they should be given –

the answer is Yes – but when to give them is still a tricky one. Clearly, the situation in which many presenters find themselves of watching their audience flicking through a sheaf of papers or studying the table on page four while they are struggling through the content of page eight, is not an ideal one. To some extent the timing of hand-outs will depend on the nature of the presentation and the familiarity of the audience with the subject matter.

A general guideline for important presentations (Yes, I know they are all important) in an ideal world would be:

Make a hand-out which outlines the content of the talk available before the presentation.

Give a detailed hand-out at the end – perhaps before the Q & A session.

In this way the audience will find it easier to pose questions since they have your choice of words in front of them and, more importantly, they will be able to refresh their memories of what was said ten days later when they have all but forgotten your message. It is undoubtedly true that messages conveyed in a foreign language are much more difficult to retain. It also means that *you* can refer to the hand-out in the succeeding weeks rather than saying: 'You remember what I said about ... '.

I am sure that I need not add that the guidelines for written communication should be strictly adhered to when you prepare your hand-outs.

Non-verbal communication

Under this heading I would include not only Body Language, by which I mean the sub/semi-conscious communication which happens more or less in spite of ourselves, but also the marginally more deliberate form of communication which I shall call *gesticulation*.

It is a cliché that an Italian with his hands tied behind his back is unable to speak. The truth is that most British and American people also gesticulate to a greater or lesser extent. The principal difference is that most of our gesticulations are meaningless and do not aid communication in any way. Generally speaking the gestures which do have a recognized meaning in our culture are to be avoided, either because they have an impolite meaning that we are aware of or because they have an impolite meaning that we are not aware of, e.g. the 'V' sign, the thumbs up, the OK sign, and so on.

However, gestures or gesticulations can be a valuable visual aid to communication when they effectively and comprehensibly mirror what we are saying. The Italians are very good at supporting what they say with clear gestures – although they also have a broad repertoire of gestures with specific meanings which we do not have access to.

A good example of a way in which gesture can effectively be used can be seen by asking someone to try to describe a spiral staircase – invariably people back up their words with a gesture. Gesture should therefore be seen as a visual aid, and the same restrictions should be placed on it.

Body language, on the other hand, is rather more universal and in my opinion should only be worried about to the extent that it may make one appear defensive or aggressive, arrogant or timorous. Being self-conscious or self-aware is useful to the presenter up to a point. Beyond that point it becomes a major distraction and is therefore counter-productive.

'Herr Doktor Schwarzkopf in charge of Quality, Ingegnere Rossi the
Production Manager – Gentlemen, this is Bob our new CEO.'

First-name terms

This topic relates more closely to business practice in different
countries; however, it is a subject which one is likely to have to
face in every meeting and presentation.

Some nationalities simply do not feel comfortable using first
names at work – even after many years of collaboration. There is
no stand-offishness implied and one should therefore not be
offended by it. Similarly, more than one European nationality is
keen on the use of titles, particularly academic titles – many of
which may appear to you and me to have been accorded or
awarded a little more readily than is our custom.

Very often individuals will expect to be addressed by this title,
whether it be the equivalent of doctor, engineer, or some other

appellation for which there is no English equivalent (like the Italian *ragioniere* or *geometrò*).

When I read in the newspapers that John Major and Helmut Kohl were already on first-name terms, I wondered whose suggestion it was and how comfortable Herr Kohl felt about it. My father worked for many years with a German who could not bring himself to be called Lutz (his first name) at work. In the end they agreed that while he would call my father by his first name, my father should address him by his initials – LR.

On a similar theme, anybody who believes that the use of *tu* and *vous* in France is easily grasped, has not understood it. The following anecdote may comfort some of you who have struggled with this problem.

After weeks of negotiations with a particular Union official, said official suggested to François Mitterand that they should use the *tu* form: *On se tutoie?* Mitterrand's response is said to have been: *Si vous voulez.*

10 Conclusions

The international business environment is no longer the habitat solely of an elite group of high fliers. Today the term *International Manager* could be used to designate a vast number of managers in a great many organizations. However, very little has been done to prepare managers for their new role. In spite of the fact that many people have asked the question: *What should we be doing to prepare or develop our managers for the new challenges facing them as a result of their increasingly plurinational exposure?* Very few, if any, authoritative answers have been given.

We might conclude from this that effective international managers are born and not made, or that the effectiveness of such managers results from the chance meeting of preparation and opportunity, like luck itself. If either of these conclusions is correct the problem of how to create effective international managers might disappear, to be replaced by the problem of how to identify them and recruit them. Unfortunately, there would not be enough of them to fill all the positions which require their skills.

The two most conspicuously successful international managers that I know personally would both admit to finding it harder it harder to function and communicate effectively in some countries than in others. This suggests to me that if they have some kind of innate or instinctive affinity with certain countries of which they are not natives, this affinity is not 100%

transferable. It should also be said that whatever instincts they may have are significantly complemented by intimate knowledge of the countries where they feel least foreign as well as, in many cases, a very high degree of fluency in the relevant languages. Such other characteristics as they share include: an unshakeable self-belief, a high tolerance of uncertainty and a polychronic ability to juggle their agendas.

The rest of us, ordinary mortals, are left with the problem of how to make ourselves, or our colleagues, more effective when dealing with clients or counterparts from other parts of the world. My firm belief that there is no intrinsic difference in the nature of such differences as exist between individuals of a single nationality or ethnic group on the one hand and between individuals who are not of the same nationality or ethnic group on the other, may be seen as a reason for optimism. We cannot forget, however, that the differences are compounded by the fact that two individuals of different nationalities will, in most cases, also have different mother tongues. Certainly this does not help matters, but since all communication is at best approximate, there is no fundamental difference between communicating with people of a different mother tongue and communicating with those whose mother tongue we share. As I suggested earlier, no two people speak English in exactly the same way and, furthermore, we cannot be completely confident about any similarities in two people's understanding of even relatively simple words – any more than we can be sure that two people who agree that a car is green, are seeing precisely the same colour/shade.

If you are a good swimmer who regularly swims across rivers and lakes, it may be helpful, when you are told that you have to swim the English Channel, to know that there is no fundamental difference between this task and others which you have frequently done, only a difference in degree of difficulty. Such reassurance is only of limited help though.

Nonetheless it does mean that the training or development required by would-be international managers does not differ radically from that required by managers without international responsibilities. Training in communication and interpersonal skills is probably the most important first step. Central to effective communication and interpersonal effectiveness is a thorough understanding of who you are. Also of paramount importance is the need to recognize that other people are different but that we do not yet know how they are different.

John Mole, the author of *Mind Your Manners*, gives as his definition of culture:

The way we do things around here.

Although I do not think that this is truly a definition of culture, it does strike me as being the most important thing to know about any new environment in which we have to work. Knowing how people work is much more useful than establishing some average cultural profile of them. Communication breakdowns generally occur because people have different ways of doing things and because these differences are not recognized. If we combine a knowledge of working practices and behaviours with an acceptance that there is more than one way of being effective, we are on the road to success.

As far as differences in culture are concerned, if we always view them simply as obstacles to overcome, we miss the opportunity of being enriched by them. If we accept that there is more than one way of thinking, more than one way of perceiving the world, we are increasing the number of options open to us. If we take the Trompenaars definition of culture:

The way in which a group of people solves problems.

By letting ourselves be enriched by other cultures we are providing ourselves with other ways of solving problems at the same time as removing the wall which prevents mutual understanding.

The fact that most people do not take potential differences between themselves and their interlocutors into account when they are trying to communicate, means that the chances of success are strictly limited. Even within a given national or ethnic group there is an argument for trying a new approach, a kind of customer-focused communication. Where international communication is concerned we need something even more radical, something which might be called Communication Process Re-engineering.

What is Communication Process Re-engineering?

Essentially, it could be explained in the following way. If, as communicators, we say that our product is Information, it is generally true that the packaging of our product says more about *us* than it does about our clients (i.e. anyone with whom we have to communicate). Clearly this has to change. Whether we are serving our clients as transmitters or receivers we have to focus on our clients and strip the communication process of any interference created by our own cultural packaging or, at the very least, ensure that our clients can see what is *product* and what is *packaging* and we ourselves must learn to distinguish between product and packaging when we are receiving. To put it another way, we have to be aware of what is value-added and what is non-value-added in terms of the communication process.

Earlier I said that the instincts of successful international managers, or at least of the ones that I know, were significantly complemented by knowledge of the countries and of the languages of their counterparts. We cannot ignore the obvious fact that it is easier to understand someone whose language we speak, even if we generally communicate with them in a language which is not their own. When I first worked with Japanese managers, many years ago, I was struck by the quizzical expression which often invaded their supposedly inscrutable faces. They would sit very still, with their head leaning slightly to one side, looking more than a little baffled as I spoke. At first I thought that they had not understood what I was saying to them; consequently I would rephrase whatever I had to say, being careful to use suitably international English. As often as not however, their bafflement did not abate. Eventually I realized that they had understood what I was saying; they were simply baffled as to why I had said it. In other words, they were trying to grasp where I was coming from, to build a context into which my words could be placed. If you never go through the process of learning a language – which implies learning a new way of thinking – it will be very difficult for you really to understand your counterparts, even if they speak almost perfect English.

Anybody who has learned more than one foreign language will tell you that the first was the most difficult. Different languages have different logics; the real difficulty lies in recognizing this fact and learning how it affects communication; having done it once, you know what to look for and even if you try to learn Mandarin Chinese, if you first learn French or Spanish or German, it will be much easier. You can learn another person in much the same way; at a higher level, by which I mean less profound, you can also learn a group of people. You should, however, guard against thinking that you can learn a whole country or ethnic group, since the level at which it can be achieved is so shallow as to be worthless.

The saying 'It takes all sorts to make a world' has become a cliché in our language, but how many of us behave as though we believed it. Even among those of us who do accept it there are

Different is not *Wrong*.

many who seem to think of all other sorts as *the BAD*, without which we would not recognize *the GOOD*.

Admitting that there are people in other places who have completely different values from ourselves, values in which they believe as strongly as – if not more than – we do, and who lead perfectly happy lives, is a step in a productive direction. Many of us who are profoundly put out by different approaches to management or business or communication issues, revel in the diversity of the world when we are on holiday in foreign countries, and genuinely appreciate the richness it brings to our lives. Anyone who has ever been delighted to discover that there is a different way of doing some everyday task is potentially an effective international manager. Recently I met a French lady who had just spent a week in a British host-family as part of a high level English course. She told me that in this family, to her initial amazement, they did not peel potatoes before boiling them. The discovery that peeling potatoes was not universally considered to be compulsory had, she told me, changed her life; she would never peel another potato. The message at work, as at play, in the office, as in the kitchen, is that assumptions are there to be questioned and that *different* is not *wrong*.

Index